THE BATTLE FOR AMERICA'S FAMILIES

The Battle
for America's
Families

A FEMINIST RESPONSE TO
THE RELIGIOUS
RIGHT

ANNE BATHURST GILSON

THE PILGRIM PRESS
Cleveland, Ohio

The Pilgrim Press, Cleveland, Ohio 44115
© 1999 by Anne Bathurst Gilson

Printed in the United States of America on acid-free paper

04   03   02   01   00   99   5   4   3   2   1

Library of Congress Cataloging-in-Publication Data

Gilson, Anne Bathurst, 1958–
    The battle for America's families : a feminist response to the religious
right / Anne Bathurst Gilson.
        p.   cm.
    Includes bibliographical references and index.
    ISBN 0-8298-1344-6 (pbk. : alk. paper)
    1. Family—Religious aspects—Christianity.   2. Feminist ethics.
3. Feminist theology.   4. Fundamentalism.   I. Title.
BT707.7.G55   1999
261.8'3585—dc21   99-30823
                                                                     CIP

To Judith,
joy to my heart and food to my soul

Contents

Acknowledgments

Many people have influenced the shape of this book. I am immensely grateful to all for feedback, support, and challenges along the way. In particular, for conversations over the years that fed into this project—to Elizabeth Alexander, Elizabeth Bounds, Karin Case, Tom F. Driver, Marvin Ellison, Ken Estey, Robin Gorsline, Beverly Wildung Harrison, Carter Heyward, Joan Martin, Margaret Mayman, Nancy Hamlin Soukup, and Barbara Weaver—I am most appreciative. Carter Heyward, Mary Ann Heyward, and Robert Heyward Jr. accompanied me to the 1998 Christian Coalition's Road to Victory Conference. Their companionship, conversational analysis, and spunk made that particular part of my research a more enjoyable undertaking. My colleague Scott Haldeman has been immensely helpful in our semiregular monthly lunches to discuss our various works in progress. He held me accountable to the importance of this project and spurred me on.

The Women and Religion Section at the American Academy of Religion provided an opportunity for a panel on family values; this marked the beginning of my research.[1] St. Mark's Episcopal Church in the Bowery (New York City) organized a lecture series on the religious right and invited several of us who were doing work on the subject to participate. That lecture fed into this book as well. During the academic year 1995–96, I was a Visiting Scholar at Episcopal Divinity School in Cambridge, Massachusetts. I am grateful for the time, space, conversations, and library resources that year provided me. In addition, the flexibility of my colleagues at RAM Associates in Washington, D.C.—especially Russ Mawn, John Pollock, Mike Sharpstene, Luann Trumbull, Dick Williams, and Chris Yaeger—permitted this book to be finished in a timely manner.

My editor, Timothy Staveteig, at The Pilgrim Press has been helpful in the acquisitions process and in the work of editing. To him, managing editor Ed Huddleston, and the staff at Pilgrim Press, I offer thanks.

While writing this book in the summer of 1998, I was planning a commitment service with my partner. The fact that I was so ensconced in reading, marking, and inwardly digesting the primary resource materials of the religious right (particularly those that denounced lesbian and gay people and defended traditional families and traditional marriage) made me feel slightly crazed. Indeed, my brain threatened to stop working. I owe a great deal to those around me at the time. They offered me comfort and urged me on to do the work I needed to do. My colleague Janet Parker in New York City suggested that I view my impending commitment service as an antidote to the intolerance of the religious right. Without those words of wisdom, I am not sure I would have been able to summon the courage to integrate those two different projects and finish the book. Other friends, Ricky Brightman, Pat Hendrickson, Sheila McJilton, Ann Philbrick, Kim Rodrigue, and Nancy Hamlin Soukup, provided welcome bouts of distraction and so helped me balance my life a bit more sanely.

To my biological family—my parents, Margaret and Dick; my brother, Rich; and my sisters, Claudia and Eileen—I am thankful. Although we do not always agree, they have been truly amazing in their capacity to stand with me along the way. My young nephew, Adam Pontious, deserves kudos as well for understanding that Aunt Anne had to work for much of his annual summer visit. To all those, near and far, who make up my extended family of choice, thank you for teaching me about the different kinds of families and the varied networks of love and support we can create for one another.

Finally, I am moved beyond words for the love and support my partner, Judith, has shown me. She helped me find time and space to write and honored this project as a priority in our lives. She understood the necessity of taking the laptop computer on the trip we took after our commitment service, and she missed a seminary board meeting to help edit. It is to her that this volume is dedicated with love and gratitude. My heart is full.

At the Crossroads

Feminism, the Religious Right, and Family Values

Is the subject of family values passé? Old news? A debate that has no current bearing on the contemporary arena of justice politics? Alas, I think not. The religious right—even after the turn of the century and the next presidential election—seems poised to carry on the rallying cry of safeguarding the sanctity of the family. From speeches to books to fund-raising literature, the religious right makes the sanctity of the family its focus. It is the organizing principle of its political strategies and the grounding tenet on which its theology is based. To dismiss this as old news is to miss the fact that the engine driving the train has family values clearly emblazoned on its side.

Because I do not subscribe to the principles of the religious right, I have been accused of having no family values. I used to object—I have family, and I have values. But members of the religious right have a particular code of behavior in mind, one that does not fit me. Indeed, to them I am the enemy. The religious right perceives itself as well as the family to be under siege from attacks by liberals (sometimes referred to as secular humanists), feminists, socialists, and lesbian and gay people. (Indeed, gay and lesbian persons receive a great deal of attention, often serving as a lightning rod for a much broader array of concerns.) This siege mentality is reflected increasingly in the language of war. The result is to draw the battle lines, shore up the defenses, and wage war over who can legitimately be included in families and thus what kind of families can be considered Christian.[1]

This book has two goals: first, to plumb the depths of the arguments of the religious right so as to be able to shape constructive responses from a feminist liberation theo-ethical perspective (rea-

2 AT THE CROSSROADS

soning that it is far better to take a well-informed constructive theological action than be forced to react without benefit of knowing the full extent of what was previously said); and second, to be able to claim the terms "values," "family," and "family values" for those of us who are critics of the religious right.

This, as one might expect, involves some redefining, some reimagining, some revisiting of what it means to be family and also of what it means to be a moral agent in contemporary society. It also involves paying attention to the economic climate in which the current debate resides. It is past time for us to be attending to the constructive tasks surrounding this issue. The circumstances grow more dire day by day as the religious right seeks to dictate both the details of family life and the acceptable moral constructs that would govern our daily lives and the welfare of the nation.

Perhaps as a symptom of our weariness of the family debate, too many of us automatically dismiss the religious right. That nonresponse accomplishes nothing. We are disdainful, defensive, downright snobby, in our belief that the arguments of the religious right do not deserve any of our attention. And here is where we make a dreadful mistake: by maintaining our disdain for the thinking of the religious right, we contribute to the polarization of the right and the left; we participate in demonizing the other side; ultimately, we fail to come up with constructive responses.

I myself am guilty of this. I believe that one reason we all do this is that we are afraid. Those of us who are excluded from and/ or do not agree with the right's definition of family are understandably defensive. We have fought too long and too hard to lose the ground we have gained. We argue that to give any time or effort to exploring the arguments of the right is to give those arguments power over us. Yet not knowing the content of those arguments is dangerous and seriously hampers our efforts to offer a constructive alternative.

In urging that we become acquainted with the thinking of the religious right, I am not championing a false unity, a premature reconciliation, or a peace without justice. Rather, we dare not underestimate the skills and power of those who place themselves in the camp of the religious right. To understand the arguments of the religious right, we do not need to accept their arguments as true; we need merely to understand that members of the religious right hold these arguments to be true.

To refuse to listen to what the right has to say is to give away our own power. We give away our power to respond. We give away our power to defend ourselves. We give away our power to take pride in our various family configurations and in our values. We give away the chance to fine-tune our own thinking and develop constructive strategies. Ultimately, we give away our theological and ethical credibility. We give away all this because we deny the humanity of those with whom we, oh, so fervently disagree. Unless we are willing to grant the humanity of our opponents, we have betrayed our commitments to a gospel-centered justice and severely jeopardized our ability to respond constructively to the issues at hand. This is not to say that we will ever agree with their arguments. That possibility is hardly likely. Nor is it likely that they will ever agree with our arguments. Rather, it means that we come to understand the concerns that fuel their fervor and the context that shapes their arguments.

When we refuse to examine the arguments of the right, we hold on to a gnawing fear of the unknown—a fear that grows day by day and further deepens the gulf between us. To be sure, the arguments of the religious right are scary. To be afraid is surely an appropriate response. We must remember, however, that these arguments have been crafted, quite deliberately, to undermine our freedom to love whom we choose, to dictate what kind of families are granted civil rights, and to control who can receive God's blessing. In spite of our denial, we are deeply affected by these arguments.

MY PERSONAL STAKE

All of us have a stake in what the religious right is saying. Mine is deeply personal. My younger sister and her family are deeply persuaded by the arguments of the right wing. She and her husband are high-ranking distributors in a Michigan-based cleaning and food products distributorship company—an organization especially known for its conservative connections. She is invested in the traditional structure of the family and, I believe, considers herself to have the perfect family.

A few years ago she told my mother that anyone who was against the religious right was an enemy of hers. This comment greatly upset my mother (who in her elder years has become quite the enthusiastic feminist) and sent chills down my spine. My sister has also been known to insist that the United States is a Christian nation and—in defense of that declaration—that Jesus was a Christian. (Imagine, if you will, our family dinner conversations.)

My knee-jerk response at having a sister of this political orientation was to insist, rather childishly, that she must have been adopted. My first response was to distance her. *She just believes these things*, I thought, *because she wants easy answers*. But the truth of the matter is that she is like me. We shared the same home, the same upbringing, the same parents, the same siblings, the same room—and whether I like it or not, the same womb. Hard as I tried, I could not deny the similarities between us; I could not deny the closeness we had had as children; I could deny neither the realities of her life nor the fact that I still wanted to be part of her life.

My second response was to listen to my sister as carefully as I could. How one understands the family is understood as the litmus test of what makes one Christian. Indeed, all the arguments of the religious right draw on or return to the well-being of the traditional family. I was by definition part of the problem because I could not say that the primary and only possible cornerstone of family life is marriage between a man and a woman and, furthermore, that this form of family is the foundation of civilization. According to the religious right, we who do not make this confession are contributors to social problems such as illegitimacy, sexually transmitted diseases, and crime.[2]

To believe as I do that families come in all shapes, sizes, and configurations makes me and others the problem. Indeed, it would be better if we went away—disappeared or were made to disappear. We are villainized, set up as scapegoats for the ills of society, and kept out of the increasingly exclusive circles of "good" Christian people. Before we know it, a holy war to defend the one true Christian way is upon us.

So there we have it. Do we continue the standoff? Do we widen the gulf between us? Do we sign up to defend our beliefs before the great holy war? Or do we get disappeared? I say the stakes are already too high; the lives of too many people are on the line; too many witch-hunts are already under way for scapegoats to sacrifice. We who cannot condone the theology, ethics, and politics of the religious right in this country must heed the urgent call to pay attention, to listen to the other side's arguments, to respond with our own carefully reasoned arguments, to reclaim the terms "family" and "values," and to construct our own theo-ethical discourse.

WHO IS THE RELIGIOUS RIGHT?

Throughout this book, the term "religious right" is used in the context of the social order of the United States in the late twentieth century to refer mostly to white evangelical Christians, despite the efforts of some groups to incorporate racial minorities into their membership. The religious right is a social movement that has increasingly focused on political action. But the religious right is not monolithic. It is a complex infrastructure of organizations with a plethora of concerns and varied approaches. As a collection of individuals and groups, it has characteristic stances. Yet it is important not to oversimplify the religious right; clearly, the components do not speak with a unified voice.

Leaders of the religious right have used various labels for their movement. Some object to the label "religious right" or "Christian right" because they believe that such labels imply that their movement is outside the political and theological mainstream. Others protest use of the term "radical right," which they see as "a bigoted code word for conservative people of faith."[3] Instead, most leaders of the religious right prefer to describe their movement as being "pro-family," having learned that naming an issue positively (for example, "pro-life" instead of "antiabortion") appeals more to the general public. However, those of us who are critics of the movement feel strongly that the agenda of the religious right is decidedly detrimental to the good of the family; therefore, we deliberately refrain from using "pro-family."

I have not included in this book any detailed exploration of the antiabortion (or pro-life) movement. Although this movement has some strong connections with the religious right, it also has a good-sized constituency among the evangelical left in this country. Also, I have not focused upon the extreme right wing, such as the Ku Klux Klan, the Christian reconstructionist movement, or militia organizations. This extreme pole of the religious right deserves more of an in-depth treatment than this book can provide.[4]

THE BOOK'S OUTLINE

Part 1 of this book—"Can Right Family Values Fix Social Wrongs?" —explores the arguments of the religious right in detail. First, chapter 1 chronicles the rise of the religious right in the late twentieth century, a rise to power that has its roots in earlier movements. In so doing, I take particular note of how the economic climate of late-twentieth-century capitalism has contributed to the rise of the movement.

Chapter 2 provides a detailed examination of some of the major groups of the Christian right—including the Promise Keepers, the Christian Coalition, Concerned Women for America, James Dobson's Focus on the Family and the political arm of that organization, the Family Research Council, as well as right-wing groups within mainline denominations—and their theological arguments.

Chapter 3 distinguishes two basic types of arguments: those based on perceived "threats" and those based on proposed "solutions." The former encompasses the so-called moral decline of civilization, the endangered status of the traditional family, and the welfare system as a threat to nation, family, and capitalism (which is often portrayed as God's "chosen" economy). The "solutions" section focuses on arguments for the male headship of the household, defense of the family, and sexual purity. The argument for how America can be assured of salvation also enters into the picture here. The emphasis of the religious right on reconciliation—especially in regard to race and gender—is detailed, as is the degree to which the rhetoric of these arguments is couched in the language of war.

Part 2, "A Feminist Response," involves two major tasks: first, a thoroughgoing analysis of the arguments of the religious right from a critical, feminist liberation theo-ethical perspective; and second, a constructive proposal for addressing concerns generated by the religious right. The first task is approached in chapter 4—"Whose Family? Whose Faith? What Justice?"—by engaging a few foundational theological assumptions that build on one another, including the creation of genders, the salvation of the family, and the one, true way of fulfilling the will of God. These basic theological assumptions serve as a foundation upon which all other arguments rely.

One particular strand of the arguments of the religious right is that of the ideology of control. This concept is explained in some depth by focusing on three manifestations of it. The first manifestation is in sexual politics. This includes foci on women's roles, issues affecting lesbian women and gay men, the defense of traditional marriage, and the promotion of traditional forms of family life. The second manifestation is in economic distributions. Here recent attacks on the welfare system are justified as a means of saving the institution of the American family—and, ultimately, as a means of saving the nation. The third manifestation of the ideology of control addresses the issue of racism and the attempts of the religious right to include racial minorities. This chapter concludes by highlighting a recent tendency of the religious right to champion a reconciliation that fails to reference justice as a primary component.

The concluding chapter 5—"Faith, Freedom, and Family"—begins by drawing on some basic theological assumptions, including our creation as children of God, the ongoing process of liberation in human history, and the notion of God-incarnate-with-us. A concept of family inclusive of the voices shunned by the religious right is drawn out by emphasizing the paradigm of justice rather than judgment. The arguments analyzed in the preceding chapters are turned around with this major paradigm shift in mind. Inclusion, not exclusion—justice, not premature reconciliation—is the order of the day, and proposals concerning sexual politics and economic well-being are presented. These responses build the groundwork for constructing models of inclusion, in which mutuality and justice are normative and where nurturing relationships—of whatever configuration—that enhance human well-being are valued. This provides a theological, ethical, and political base for exploring what "family" might look like beyond traditional boundaries and for developing resources to face the crises we meet on a daily basis in an unjust social order.

The book concludes with a discussion of the moral agency we must claim as justice-loving people of faith. Acknowledging the personal nature of the culture war taking place between those on the religious right who uphold an exclusive concept of family values and those of us who insist on justice-centered concepts of "family" and "values," the fact that we live in an in-between time of great uncertainty is explored. How do we even begin to answer the concerns of those who maintain that anything less than conformity to the traditional marriage formula puts our entire civilization at risk? How do we address our sisters and brothers who are so terrified of change that they see those who are not like them—even if they are their own flesh and blood—as threatening their well-being, even their very survival? Finally, strategies for meeting the challenges are proposed by detailing three stages of action: being unrepentant, being of good faith, and cultivating a holy impatience.

THE BOOK'S APPROACH

The methodological resources I employ in this book are drawn from three intersecting traditions: social construction theory, liberation theologies, and feminist liberation theology. The first, social construction theory, means that I approach the task before me understanding that many of our beliefs about gender, sexuality, and family are constructs of society and are not primarily biologically imputed. (On this basic methodological score, I depart dramatically from the assumptions of the religious right.) Rather, our notions of gender, sexuality, and family are shaped by a panoply of interconnecting social institutions and forces, including economic, familial, religious, political, and community norms. Social construction theory is by definition a relational theory. On this merit alone, it is the perfect methodological companion for liberation theologies in general and feminist liberation theologies in particular. I do not believe that social construction theory accounts for all of our formation around gender and sexuality (for instance, we cannot totally dismiss the influence of biological factors); however, I do believe the theory has a great deal to do with the discussion at hand: primarily, discussing the roles of men and women in the context of the family.

The second resource is the decades-old tradition of liberation theologies. This tradition has been formative to my approach to the doing of theology. I owe much to liberation theologians from Latin America, Africa, and Asia, as well as African American, Hispanic, and American Indian liberation theologians in this country. The presuppositions underlying their theological work—that God is on the side of those who are oppressed, that God is not a God who takes "His" wrath out on those with whom God is displeased, and that God is a God who seeks justice and seeks our participation in making justice in the world—inform the basis of my work. Over the years, the work of these theologians has raised my consciousness, sharpened my analysis, helped me to see the interconnections among all of us who live on this planet, and fueled my desire to make justice in this world. In the midst of such struggles comes the knowledge that no one of us is truly alone. All of our struggles are connected, and while at times we may not do a good job of making those connections, nevertheless we are full of the knowledge that those connections are there, that there is always more work to be done to make justice, and most important of all, that there is hope for the future.

The third methodological resource—that of feminist liberation theology—is the stream in which I place myself most directly and which grows out of social construction theory and liberation theologies. Feminist liberation theology is a theology that seeks to empower women to hear one another into speech,[5] raises up the voices of all women across all lines of difference, and focuses on taking racism, classism, heterosexism, able-bodyism, ageism, and nationalism as seriously as it takes sexism. In short, feminist liberation theology differs from its foremother feminist theology, which based its analysis primarily on sexism.

These three methodological resources, then—social construction theory, liberation theologies, and feminist liberation theology—shape the analysis and concerns that I bring to the task ahead. As such, they form the heart of this book.

While I believe strongly that our methodological questions must be well grounded in our belief systems, I maintain that we must open ourselves and allow our belief systems to be challenged by the questions of others. I believe as well that our theological methodologies must allow us to dig deeply, to uncover the roots of what has gone before so that we might understand the questions of the present.[6] Our methodologies must also allow us to put down roots, to value the places in which we live, the traditions that have been passed on to us, the struggles of those who have gone before us. And our work cannot stop there. As comforting as it may be, we cannot dwell exclusively on our roots and on the process of putting down roots. Our rooting is essential to the doing of theology (without roots we would wither and die), but we must also be able to branch out, to open ourselves to understanding and hearing the experiences, questions, and passions of others as we all seek to create together a justice-love[7] that overcomes oppression and alienation.[8]

MY SOCIAL LOCATION

As a feminist liberation theo-ethicist, I believe that, in the doing of theology, I must situate myself in a particular social context, giving the reader clues to the biases I bring to this project. Those who read theology and commentary on social issues need to know where the author stands and what social influences have most shaped the author's work. The sort of knowledge that can be conveyed is, by necessity, limited, but at least it gives the reader a starting point for beginning to understand the author's position. And the author is always free to be selective about the information she or he discloses. Nevertheless, before proceeding, let me claim a few essential details.

A few of my proclivities have already been made known through the methodological resources I employ. The others include a few hard facts: I am a white person in a racist society, a middle-class person in a society that treats its poor people rather disdainfully, an overeducated person in a society in which ever higher and more technological levels of education are necessary to "succeed" economically, a female person in a sexist social order, and a lesbian person in a society that is increasingly torn asunder over the threat or, conversely, the opportunity that lesbian women, gay men, and bisexual people pose for traditional understandings of gender roles and the entwined institutions of family and marriage. I am also one who deeply loves, learns from, and actively engages my biological family, my life partner, my extended family of close friends, and my family of four-footed creatures. This constellation of family feeds me, teaches me, challenges me, and loves me. This family is ever present as I delve further into the complicated subject of "family."

As I finished this book on the religious right, three critical events were taking place. First, the bishops of the worldwide Anglican communion (of which I, as a cradle Episcopalian, am a part) were having their once-every-decade meeting in Lambeth, England. They passed resolutions denouncing the ordinations of self-affirming lesbian and gay people as well as the blessing of same-gender unions. Saddened by the turn of events at Lambeth, I vow to celebrate love and commitment wherever they might be found. Second, my partner, Judith, and I had a blessing of our "same-gender union"—as it turned out, two days before the close of the bishops' Lambeth Conference. Strengthened and blessed by the power of our gathered communities, I vow to remember that we are not just two women who love each other; we are two women with a wealth of familial communities, connected to a wider movement for social justice. Third, two weeks before this book was due, our beloved twelve-year-old gray cat, Ethel (aka the ruler of the universe), was dying of sinus cancer. Honored by her deigning to share her life with me, I vow to hold up the critical roles of animal companions in our family lives.

Why reveal these details? These facts, as one might imagine, have quite a bit to do with how I feel about the subject matter at hand. To pretend that they did not, to say, for instance, that I was "objective" in my approach to the questions raised in this book, that I was not daily torn by the debate swirling around me, would be to hide the experiences that have shaped me and to conceal deliberately the interests and passions I bring to the discussion. The particularities of my familial and ecclesiastical connections cannot help but influence how I approach the sociopolitical and theological issues embedded in the discourse about families. I hope that the readers, too, will consider what the details of their lives mean as they consider the topic before us. To the reader: this topic is difficult to engage. Be prepared to have your sensibilities offended, your hackles raised, and your heart engaged. How do your understanding and experiences of "family" influence the questions you ask, the presuppositions you hold, and the dreams you have for the future? What are your fondest hopes for the future of "family" in this society? What are your fears? What are you willing to risk in the pages ahead?

PART 1

Can Right Family Values Fix Social Wrongs?

———

1

The Roots of the Religious Right

I never thought that the government would go so far afield, I
never thought the politicians would become so untrustworthy, I
never thought the courts would go so nuts to the left, and I
misjudged the quality of government that we have. Our lack of
involvement is probably one of the reasons why the country's in
the mess it is in. We have defaulted by failing to show up for the
fight.[1]

Jerry Falwell

The religious right in this country was not created ex nihilo, and
it is not a recent phenomenon. Indeed, manifestations of the religious right can be traced back to the turn of the twentieth century.

The religious right is not monolithic; it never has been and
never will be. It is made up of a variety of interest groups, which
in turn focus on a myriad of issues. As is the case in any movement, it is difficult—if not downright impossible—to find agreement across the board. Furthermore, people experience a great
deal of confusion surrounding what to call the religious right: the
terms "evangelical" and "fundamentalist" are thrown around a lot.
In fact, these terms are often used interchangeably. However,
evangelicals are not happy about being grouped with fundamentalists, and fundamentalists are even more unhappy about being
confused with evangelicals whom they perceive as being too liberal. Although the two groups share some basic theological positions regarding salvation, they differ in the degree to which they
are open to dialogue. Evangelicals are more concerned with dem-
onstrating the intellectual integrity of their positions, are open to
dialogue with other denominations, and are often more attentive

to the social mandate of the gospel.[2] They hold in common with fundamentalists (1) a belief in the inerrancy of the Bible, (2) the necessity of a faith experience of Jesus as the one and only Savior and Lord, (3) a commitment to converting the rest of the world to the Christian faith, and (4) a distrust of modern theology, especially as it pertains to the interpretation of biblical materials.[3]

When describing themselves, fundamentalists begin with the declaration that they are saved, have turned their lives over to Jesus, and have been baptized in the Holy Spirit. The central point of their mission is to seek converts and save lost souls. Their goal is to persuade the masses that "eternity in heaven is better than the eternal damnation that surely awaits the unsaved."[4] In particular, premillennialist fundamentalists believe in the importance of saving as many souls as possible before the rapture, for (as they teach) when the rapture comes, all those who are saved will be thrown up in the air with Jesus and in a twinkling of an eye will disappear. Any whose doctrine is impure and any who are not saved will be left behind; even the Holy Spirit will depart from the earth. Seven years of tribulation will follow, during which Satan will work through the antichrist. Only after the battle of Armageddon, when the antichrist has been killed and Satan has been banished for a thousand years, will Jesus return and rule a new heaven and a new earth. With stakes like these, premillennialist fundamentalists are motivated to undertake the saving of as many individual souls as possible with a great deal of fervor.

Some fundamentalists see themselves as postmillennialists. They believe that Christ will come again after a thousand-year period of peace. Christians first have to do all they can to establish this period of peace. Working to hasten the second coming of Jesus is all-important; working for Christian peace and justice in society is essential. Thus, politics is a central duty in the life of a postmillennialist, fundamentalist Christian.

Conversely, if one were to describe oneself as a premillennialist —one who believed that the state of the world would deteriorate before Christ would come again to rescue the true believers—then engagement in politics would be useless. Indeed, any involvement in the secular world at all could only detract from one's focus on staying ideologically pure. The top priority for premillennialist fundamentalists is to keep as separate from the world of sin as possible in order to avoid being tempted. Premillennialist tendencies breed an intense aversion to political involvement that leaders of various incarnations of the religious right throughout the twentieth century have had to work hard to overcome.[5]

In the late nineteenth century, when Protestant fundamentalism began to form, leaders of this movement were concerned that what was happening around them, both in theological venues and in the secular world, was increasingly contrary to what they saw as being true to the one and only faith. At the turn of the twentieth century, leaders of this new movement based their arguments on the centrality of a few doctrines and insisted that particular behavioral norms necessarily followed from those doctrines.[6] As the century turned, fundamentalists gained in strength and numbers as they built a movement concerned with resisting theological modernism. Part of that resistance was to the growth of the Social Gospel movement. Some fundamentalists saw the Social Gospel movement as denying the fact that Christians should stay as far away from worldly influences as possible while they waited for the end time and for Christ to rescue them. Revivalists, such as Dwight Moody, responded by spearheading a conservative crusade "to defend evangelical values against the forces of liberalism and modernism."[7] This agenda included marching onward to do battle against the evils of evolution and the heretical theology of the Social Gospel movement.

The Social Gospel movement did indeed represent a change in soteriology—more commonly known as salvation history—for its proponents began to believe in history itself: that is, that this world was the *only* sphere in which meaningful human action could take place, and therefore, all were called to act in this world. Furthermore, one's actions could no longer be justified by otherworldly, spiritual, private criteria, but were held up against the criteria of a secular, humanistic social order.[8]

Walter Rauschenbusch (1861–1918), perhaps the best known among the theologians of the Social Gospel movement, gave up his post as a Baptist seminary professor and took a church in the Hell's Kitchen neighborhood of New York City—a place particularly known for its corner on human suffering. He believed that it was God's will for people of faith to be involved in the politics of the day, particularly those that affected the disadvantaged masses of humanity. The Social Gospel, for him, required a push for the creation of justice in all areas of life and provided a clarion call to wake up the churches.[9]

The Social Gospel movement was critical of a capitalist economy. Attention was shifted from justifying the rise of industrialism and the concomitant gain of social standing to expressing concern for the well-being of the masses, especially the workers, immigrants, and others who were being run over by the wheels of industrial progress. Rauschenbusch insisted, "The supremacy of Profit in Capitalism stamps it as a mammonistic organization with which Christianity can never be content."[10]

Darwin's theory of evolution was another factor that led to the Social Gospelers' focus on historical processes. It represented a direct challenge to biblical literalism and to the traditional understandings of both human and divine nature. Indeed, it was one of the primary causes of the friction between fundamentalists and modernists—particularly in terms of how Christians should respond to the new science. Fundamentalists always opposed any science that might contradict their literal understanding of God's creation of the universe and of human life. Darwin's theory of evolution posed a threat to the beliefs they held dear: "that humans inhabited a world created suddenly, perhaps literally in one week, by God; that humans themselves were all descended from a single pair, Adam and Eve, who were subjects of divine creation and were made in the image of God."[11] The fact that some Christians began accepting the theory of evolution, and furthermore that they found the literalism of fundamentalism embarrassing, created a schism that was increasingly based on class and education. Those who had access to educational resources—that is, those who had money—were exposed to new ways of thinking about the origins of the universe and of human life, as well as new ways of interpreting Scripture. Colleges and universities were obvious places to wage the battle of creationism versus evolution; public schools quickly became another site.

The infamous Scopes trial of 1925 took place after Tennessee passed an antievolution law and the American Civil Liberties Union encouraged biology teacher John Scopes to test it. With Clarence Darrow and John Scopes on one side and former secretary of state and perennial presidential hopeful William Jennings Bryan and the antievolutionists on the other side, the first shots were fired. Bryan, convinced that the teaching of evolution was having deleterious moral effects on the U.S. social order, brought literal interpretations of the Bible to bear against what he saw as an immoral, heretical evolutionary theory. He laid all the ills of the U.S. social order at the feet of the teaching of evolution and suggested it would "be better to destroy every other book ever written, and save just the first three verses of Genesis."[12] Darrow presented new understandings and the latest scientific theories of the intellectual elite. As history tells it, Bryan and the fundamentalists won the legal skirmish, but did so at a great cost to the culture. Historians Martin Marty and R. Scott Appleby observe that the fundamentalists got "a bad name for obscurantism and folksy ignorance, and the image of [them as] hillbillies and backwoods inhabitants stuck."[13] Unexpectedly, within a week after the trial, Bryan died.

Though the fundamentalists won the trial, their reputation was tarnished. The Scopes trial was a watershed event: it was all too clear that America was no longer a so-called Christian nation. The ultimate authority of the Bible was effectively challenged, and the church was no longer in control of the educational institutions. It was also apparent that the conservative religious movement had decided to seek a divorce from mainline Protestantism on the grounds of irreconcilable differences. Mainline Protestantism was increasingly accommodating theology (as the era of historical criticism was ushered in) to the changes in the social order.[14] These trends, combined with the failure of Prohibition, led to what historians have called the Great Reversal—the movement for political and religious reordering in the early twentieth century during which fundamentalists and other evangelicals dissociated themselves from social reform movements and fled from the political scene. Politics, after all, was a fruitless endeavor and only distracted true Christians from concerns of a purely spiritual nature, or so they told themselves at the time.

And so it remained for a while. During the Great Reversal, many fundamentalists, frustrated by the seemingly endless ecclesiastical battles over what was fundamental to Christian belief, left mainline denominations to form their own denominations. While they were at it, they founded their own schools, seminaries, and publishing houses; in addition, they took advantage of the new medium for communication and produced religious radio shows as a way of evangelizing the populace. The focus was on spiritual revival. Billy Sunday, one of the earlier revival preachers, sermonized against such political pariahs as immigrants, social reformers, and socialists. "If I had my way with these ornery wild-eyed socialists and IWW's," pontificated Sunday, "I would stand them up before a firing squad."[15] He asserted that religion always expressed itself in patriotism and insisted that anyone willing to make an effort could succeed. Sunday abhorred the Social Gospel promulgated by the Federal Council of Churches (the forerunner of the National Council of Churches) and characterized such theological efforts as "godless social service nonsense," which were "un-American in motivation and result."[16]

In the 1930s, radio evangelists issued warning after warning against godless communism while urging their listeners to uphold the Christian virtues (which presumably did not include generous feelings toward communism, socialism, labor unions, the progressive social reforms of FDR, or immigrants). In opposition to the liberal, ecumenical body, the World Council of Churches (denounced by its opponents as Communist), religious conservatives formed the American Council of Christian Churches. Billy James Hargis, organizer of the Christian Crusade, distributed films such as *Communism on the Map*, *Ronald Reagan on the Welfare State*, and *The Truth about Communism* (narrated by Reagan).[17] During this apparent retreat from politics, organizations on the religious right were hard at work building an impressive infrastructure that would serve them well in later decades.

After World War II, the religious right was again reunited, spurred back into the public arena of politics by an intense and all-consuming fear of the Communist threat. Not only was the religious right back to addressing a political issue, but it joined with the political right and quickly rallied to support Senator Joseph McCarthy in his efforts to rid the United States of "the Red Menace." Such a coalition was believed to be necessary if the crusade to save the country was to succeed. In this climate, in 1954, Congress voted to insert the words "under God" in the Pledge of Allegiance as a way of conveying the critical role of religion—namely, Christianity—in the fight against godless communism.

During this period, fundamentalist preacher Carl McIntire, for whom purity of doctrine was of ultimate concern, gained prominence as he insisted that the well-being of the country rested on a return to the "old-time" Christian values upon which the nation had been founded. This return, he warned, would not be easy because of the Communist conspiracy afoot in the land. He declared the National Council of Churches to be a hotbed of communism and believed that the Revised Standard Version of the Bible (just published in 1952) was a Communist undertaking. The Supreme Court decisions on prayer in the public school system were also part of the Communist plot to sabotage the Christian foundation of the United States.[18] The Christian Anti-Communism Crusade actively opposed Medicare because it was "socialized medicine"; the group was adamant that any sort of sex education program would decay the country's morals, thus making the country even more vulnerable to a Communist takeover.[19] In response to the liberalism of the Federal Council of Churches, McIntire formed the American Council of Christian Churches (ACCC) in 1941; seven years later he founded the International Council of Christian Churches (ICCC), whose sole purpose was to stand in opposition to the World Council of Churches.

Billy James Hargis, a fervent anti-Communist, fundamentalist minister, was a prominent leader of the movement and, in 1951, founded the Christian Crusade. To this day, he believes that communism continues to be a threat to the country and, moreover, that the liberal media are colluding to keep that threat hidden. As recently as August 1994, he asserted that communism, in spite of its collapse in Central and Eastern Europe, "is making a dramatic, secret comeback. . . . There is a Red threat and it is alive and thriving."[20]

In the 1950s, Billy Graham, usually a reluctant participant in the politics of the day, declared that the only political issue worthy of mention from the pulpit was communism, which he saw as being "anti-God, anti-Christ, and anti-American." He believed that communism represented a battle between the antichrist and Christ and was an issue that deserved the attention and action of faithful Christian people. Only the truth of the gospel of Christ could provide the "antidote for the poisonous venom of Sovietism." If America did not heed the warning, it would "plunge into the dark abyss of totalitarian despair and gloom, and ultimate annihilation." If, however, America embraced the right and followed the Christian way, he predicted that the country "well might be entering the greatest economic and spiritual renaissance that modern man has known."[21]

The struggle for civil rights in the sixties brought criticism from those on the religious right. Jerry Falwell, commenting on President Johnson's civil rights reform, remarked that "it should be considered civil wrongs rather than civil rights" and believed it was a horrendous violation of both human rights and property rights. He deeply criticized those liberal clergy, both black and white, who were involved in the struggle for civil rights, asserting that the only role clergy should play was that of making Christ known to the world. Falwell declared that his belief in the Bible would keep him from doing anything that might be construed as "political" (including fighting communism). Preaching the gospel was the only acceptable public role for a member of the clergy, he maintained. After all, ministers were not "called to be politicians, but to be soul winners."[22]

During the decades of the 1960s and 1970s, while the war in Vietnam raged; African Americans struggled for their civil rights; feminists organized; U.S. cities, caught in the travail of racism, burned in the midst of rioting; John F. Kennedy, Robert F. Kennedy, and Martin Luther King Jr. were assassinated; hippies rebelled against the values of their parents; and the Supreme Court ruled that abortions were legal, fundamentalists looked around and began to take stock of the situation. They organized around the threat that secular humanism posed to the moral fiber of the nation. To them, secular humanism represented every imaginable sin and probably every unimaginable sin as well. Secular humanists, like the Communists who preceded them, were supposed to have infiltrated the court and school systems and to be in control of the media. In addition, the United Nations and even at times the State Department and Department of Education were denounced as being under the control of secular humanists. According to the religious right, secular humanists were about the business of undermining Christianity. In 1986, Pat Robertson charged that the "small elite of lawyers, judges, and educators . . . [have] taken the Holy Bible from our young and replaced it with the thoughts of Charles Darwin, Karl Marx, Sigmund Freud, and John Dewey."[23]

The overwhelming threat that secular humanism apparently posed to the social order inspired the religious right once again to come forward and take action. As had happened before, leaders of the religious right had to convince a leery constituency that it was God's will to be active in politics instead of remaining separate from the sinful world. The time had come, once again, to convene the councils and take action. On July 4, 1976, Jerry Falwell capitalized on the Bicentennial Celebration of the United States and brought together patriotism and Christian faith. He did his best, in an intriguing reversal of his own theology, to convince the faithful to take action for the sake of God's Kingdom: "The idea that religion and politics don't mix was invented by the Devil to keep Christians from running their own country. . . . If [there is] any place in the world we need Christianity, it's in Washington. And that's why preachers long since need to get over that intimidation forced upon us by liberals, that if we mention anything about politics, we are degrading our ministry."[24] While blaming equally the devil and the liberals for the religious right's lack of involvement in politics, Falwell successfully convinced people to fight to take back the country. He urged fundamentalist Christians forward into battle, proclaiming that it was "time for an 'army' of spiritually concerned men to lead America the right way."[25]

Early in 1979, Falwell established the Moral Majority, which focused on registering conservative voters and disseminating information in the form of voters' guides designed to "educate" voters. Around the same time, the organizations Religious Roundtable, Concerned Women for America, and Christian Voice were founded. The latter highlighted the voting records of members of Congress who failed to measure up to the high moral standards of good Christian people. In August 1980, the Religious

Roundtable sponsored the National Affairs Briefing—a meeting of ten thousand fundamentalist clergy in Dallas, Texas. Ronald Reagan, the only candidate in attendance, delighted the gathering by announcing that "he also believed that evolution was only a theory."[26] Reagan added, "I know that you cannot endorse me, but I endorse you and everything you do."[27]

With the beginning of the Reagan presidency, it was apparent that a new incarnation of the religious right had, indeed, come forth. Although the coalition of groups in the religious right, which included fundamentalists, conservative-minded evangelicals, and Pentecostals, had theological disagreements, they nevertheless inspired people to take action by arguing that contemporary U.S. culture was so utterly corrupt that their only option was to band together, get involved, and do everything possible to save the country.[28] David Noebel, who was involved in the Christian right in the 1950s as well as the 1960s, denounced those who did not involve themselves in the political struggle, declaring that "a special place in hell is being reserved for people who believe in walking down the middle of the political and religious road. It will be their privilege to fry with Eleanor Roosevelt and Adlai Stevenson."[29]

The infrastructure of the religious right, begun in earlier years under other circumstances, was an invaluable asset in mobilizing the faithful. It had become a great deal more sophisticated, of course. (For instance, between 1965 and 1983, the number of students matriculating to fundamentalist and evangelical Christian schools increased sixfold.)[30] During the 1970s, with the growth of television ministries (despite the scandals involving Jimmy Swaggart and Jim and Tammy Bakker), the infrastructure expanded exponentially, and impressive amounts of money were raised.[31] This decade also witnessed the births of the supposedly nonpartisan Moral Majority, along with organizations such as the American Coalition for Traditional Values. Attention was focused primarily on electing conservatives to office in order to undermine the liberal power base. To that end, grassroots organizing was the name of the game. Falwell had come to believe that the pulpit was a central communication vehicle in the organizing of the political movement and urged pastors to have members of their congregation fill out letters, during church services, to be sent to state representatives protesting the Equal Rights Amendment (ERA). Having once vehemently denounced Christians who involved themselves in the political arena, Falwell cheered on the masses and urged that further action be taken against those who might pose a threat to the salvation of America, including homosexuals, abortionists, pornographers, atheists, secular humanists, Marxists, and feminists.[32]

Ironically, the organizers of the religious right in this era focused on copying the strategies of the old left. After all, the stakes were too high to lose. Grassroots organizing and general protest actions spurred on the cause. In the words of Paul Weyrich, founder of the Committee for the Survival of a Free Congress and widely touted as "the godfather of social conservatives,"[33] "This is really the most significant battle of the age-old conflict between good and evil, between the forces of God and forces against God, that we have seen in our country."[34]

The battles generated in the 1970s and 1980s over the Equal Rights Amendment and the growth of the feminist movement inspired fundamentalist women, who declared that women did not need to be liberated in order to take political action. Women such as Phyllis Schlafly rose to the forefront of the movement, claiming that patriarchy was the will of God and was actually beneficial for women; furthermore, women of the religious right joined their male counterparts in asserting that feminism was responsible for the deterioration of the family. They formed coalitions with other groups of the religious right to ensure the defeat of the ERA, convinced that, if it passed, the insistence on the independent personhood of women would destroy the male-female roles mandated by Scripture and would result in the legitimation of same-gender relationships. These women preferred the conventional, well-defined gender roles to those that might lead women to take seriously and celebrate their independence as unique persons, equal, in all respects, to men. One female opponent of the ERA, when faced with this possibility, remarked frankly, "I don't care to be a person."[35]

Pat Robertson's description of feminism captures much of the feeling of the religious right concerning the subject: "The feminist agenda is not about equal rights for women. . . . It is about a socialist, anti-family political movement that encourages women to leave their husbands, kill their children, practice witchcraft, destroy capitalism, and become lesbians."[36] Women of the religious right heartily concur, firmly believing that the changes wrought by feminists have been for the worse and that feminists, by spreading lies about the oppression of women, have succeeded only in destroying family life and jeopardizing the future of the nation.

THE ECONOMICS OF FAMILY LIFE AND THE FATE OF THE AMERICAN DREAM

The discourse regarding family values is based in large part on the myth of a country where anyone can succeed and all can share in the riches spawned by a thriving capitalist economy. The American Dream has fueled the yearnings of millions of people and widely propagated the expectation that there is no reason why all people, regardless of whatever hardships they have faced, cannot attain financial stability in the form of a house cum white picket fence, hardworking husband, stay-at-home wife, and 2.4 children so long as they work hard. Anyone, so the saying goes, ought to be able to pull oneself up by one's bootstraps.

In the aftermath of World War II, the United States had the sole surviving industrialized economy in the world. Americans were able to take advantage of the opportunities the postwar economic boom afforded them and make progress down the road to the American Dream. It was a unique time of prosperity in American economic history, for prior to that time most people's financial lives were none too stable on even a daily basis.

The dramatic postwar rise in the standard of living trickled down to the populace in general and enhanced the personal finances of millions of Americans. Christian social ethicist Beverly Wildung Harrison noted that these economic gains fed the "myth of classlessness" inherent to the American Dream and shored up belief in a country where anyone could aspire to and attain a secure, if not prosperous, financial life. However, since the presidency of Richard Nixon, she explained, the right has told a different story of how these economic gains came about. They connect

American prosperity with "the perennial fruit of unbridled 'free enterprise'" and thus reason that capitalism has God's stamp of approval. Harrison also pointed out that every positive change in the living standards of Americans is directly related to the acceleration of national wealth and is not due to the redistribution of economic gains, as some politicians would prefer their constituencies to believe.[37]

As we approach the turn of the century, however, the economic climate in the United States is one in which the rich have become richer and the poor have become poorer. Pat Robertson recently declared, "Capitalism has triumphed in our world."[38] It is no longer possible for people to pull themselves up by their bootstraps. Increasing numbers of people do not even own a pair of boots. Even if they did have boots replete with bootstraps, capitalism has mutated to such a degree that the opportunities to pull oneself up by one's own bootstraps are fewer and fewer in number. The wealth of the richest 1 percent of United States citizens is now nearly as much as that of the bottom 95 percent of the entire population of the United States combined.[39] In the city of New York, the income gap between the rich and the poor is more extreme than in Guatemala. In 1990, the Census Bureau recorded that 40 percent of all children whose families were headed by someone under the age of thirty were living in poverty. This figure included one out of four children in white families and one out of five children in married-couple families. The statistics would be even more grim if the work hours of white middle-class women had not increased so dramatically over the last decade. What, in God's name, has happened to the American Dream?

Clearly, the American Dream is not what it used to be. The economy, as we know all too well, is not what it once was, and the alleged trickle down of gains in national wealth has dried up. Economic gains are fewer and farther between. Mostly, they are nonexistent. These days the few economic gains rarely show up in the finances of the common family. Indeed, thousands of family farms and businesses, once thought to be secured by hard work and to be an inheritance for the next generation, have been lost to agribusiness and corporate enterprises. Young people who go deeply into debt to finance an education are no longer assured of upward mobility. The economy is becoming more and more centralized and capital intensive. As Harrison pointed out, the labor market is segmenting—that is, producing few high-income jobs and many low-income jobs, which more and more come without the traditional benefits won by those who fought so hard to organize labor.[40] No longer is home ownership guaranteed; one's retirement years are less and less secure. Of course, this is news only to those of us who are white and of the middle class. Those of African American, Hispanic, Asian, or American Indian descent and all those who are poor fail to be surprised by the often devastating personal ramifications of late monopoly capitalism.

We currently find ourselves in this economic climate—what Harrison terms the "culture of capitalism."[41] Those who have discovered that upward mobility is but an illusion, those who are downsized out of a job, those who have spent tens of thousands of dollars on an education and are chronically underemployed, and those whose job skills have been outmoded by technological advances are faced with the discomfiting question of what has gone wrong. The rate of personal bankruptcies has skyrocketed in the last decade. Folks who are lucky enough to have found work that pays well are caught in the trap of having to work more and more hours to pay for their inflated standard of living, with less and less time to enjoy life. Indeed, this has become a society in which we hear more about consumer rights than about issues affecting the well-being of the citizenry. This state of affairs breeds an overwhelming sense of isolation in which each individual feels at fault for the failure to thrive economically.

Appeals to family values by the religious right are based on the premise that any challenge to this economic system threatens the home front—seemingly the last haven from the madcap pace and draining demands of contemporary life. Indeed, as we shall see below, late monopoly capitalism threatens the very survival of family and community life. Appeals to family values, invoking a picture of a home where all is right with the world, reinforce a longing for a simpler, more carefree time. No note is taken of the actual day-to-day lived realities of many people in which the home is as likely to be a scene of a domestic battleground, in which women and children are not safe, and in which economic stress takes a sometimes fatal toll on one's most intimate relationships. Yet appeals to family values fill a hunger in people who more and more find themselves bewildered by their growing powerlessness. They long for a feeling of safety, an ordered world, a context over which they might exercise some control. The notion of the sanctity of the family promises to bestow a balm on the wounds created by the necessity of participation in the workforce of capitalism. The sanctity of the home promises the restorative comforting touch of Mother.

As the economy has become more industrialized and capital intensive, it has also reconstituted the boundaries between the private and the public worlds. The institution of the family increasingly intersects both worlds, and as a result, family life has become much more of a public affair. Social ethicist Elizabeth Bounds suggests that this intersection of the private and the public worlds plays a critical role in terms of how the role of the family in contemporary society is evaluated and what moral expectations are subsequently placed on the family. As such, the public/private dichotomy cannot be neglected in any discussion of family values.[42]

Historically, women have been relegated to the private world of the home and family and systematically excluded from the public world. Women, as the caretakers of the home, guarded it as a retreat from the coldhearted and cruel public world, which their men had to traverse. With the rise of the feminist movement, the private world of home and family has become much more visible in the public arena as the issues of violence against women and children, the economic value of household labor, reproductive rights, and the financial and legal vulnerability of women are brought to the attention of the general public. The increased participation of white middle-class women in the workplace (where poor women were already) has resulted in a challenge to the notion that women must depend upon the breadwinning capabilities of men. Bounds points out that this has also resulted in the foray of capitalism into all areas of life, including the private.[43] This has been especially true in terms of the political manipulations of the welfare bureaucracy; financially vulnerable women find that their private lives become fodder for a public generally hostile to welfare recipients.

We cannot consider the family apart from the public sphere. In our analysis of family values, we cannot continue to separate the private from the public, the hearth from the workplace. Nor can we neglect a thoroughgoing analysis of how economic factors affect the discourse regarding the family. The family is not and never has been separate from the various forces that shape society. The view that the family is the last sanctuary from the dangerous public world and, furthermore, that women must safeguard that sanctuary is in part based on the fear of the loss of a carefully ordered and well-controlled political and moral sphere. The clarion call of family values can be viewed then both as a backlash against the growing participation of women in the public arena and as a response to continuing changes in the social order.[44]

The strong support of the religious right for a free market, capitalist economy is connected with its disdainful rejection of communism and socialism. Both are stamped as idolatrous and are deemed "incompatible with a Christian understanding of humanity and historical destiny."[45] Socialism, as evil number four on Jerry Falwell's 1980 hit list of the evils threatening America, has been defined as being anti-God, and capitalism has been championed as "God's plan for our economy."[46] Even though Pat Robertson admits that capitalism can be both abused and abusive, he believes that it is the system that is "most conducive to freedom, most in accord with human nature, and most closely related to the Bible."[47] Deeply concerned over the failure of mainline denominational bodies to claim democracy and capitalism as normative, the religious right continues to label entities such as the National Council of Churches as Communist sympathizers. Richard Neuhaus has noted, "The leadership of mainline Protestantism cannot contribute to the moral legitimation and definition of the American [Dream] because, when all is said and done, it no longer believes in that [Dream]."[48]

Perhaps that sentiment best expresses the gist of the matter: the American Dream has gone bankrupt. We can all agree—no matter which perspective we hold—that something is terribly wrong. The exact diagnosis and prescription for recovery, however, are subject to a great deal of debate.

THE TEAR IN THE MORAL FABRIC

As we have seen, those of the religious right who believe that Jesus will not come again until peace has reigned for a thousand-year period (postmillennialists) are those who are most likely to be involved in politics. The religious right in the twentieth century has entered the political arena only when the survival of the social order appeared to be at stake. Although many of the political battles seemed to be over perceived threats posed by modernists, liberals, socialists, Communists, feminists, or secular humanists, and over issues such as evolution, the "Communist threat," prayer in schools, sexuality, gender roles, abortion, and birth control, most fundamentalists have understood the issue of ultimate concern to be about the very survival of Christian civilization.[49] At different points, various events have been identified as causing the downslide of American values. One author asserted that 1963, the year the Supreme Court banned school prayer, marked the beginning of the end. A "plague of social ills," including "teen pregnancy, illiteracy, drug use, crime, out-of-wedlock births, and welfare dependency all have skyrocketed since America's leaders decided that God should play no role in her governance."[50] That much of the literature of the religious right is laced with references to the moral decay of the nation and its imminent demise is, therefore, no surprise. Movement leaders exhort their constituencies to do everything possible to save the soul of the nation. Jerry Falwell expressed the urgent need to stem the rising tide of "moral decay" crushing American society, urging good Christian people to make the commitment so desperately needed in order to save the soul of the nation.

> In light of our present moral condition, we as a nation are quickly approaching the point of no return. There can be no doubt that the sin of America is severe. We are literally approaching the brink of national disaster. Many have exclaimed, "If God does not judge America soon, He will have to apologize to Sodom and Gomorrah." In almost every aspect of our society, we have flaunted our sinful behavior in the very face of God Himself. . . . We have become one of the most blatantly sinful nations of all time. We dare not con-

tinue to excuse ourselves on the basis of God's past blessing in our national heritage.[51]

The call to save the country from the ravages of secular sin is the rallying cry heard most frequently. America may have been blessed and protected by God at the beginning of its history, but that blessing and protection, according to the religious right, can no longer be counted upon.

Well-known televangelist, host of *The 700 Club*, and past presidential candidate, Pat Robertson describes this elect nature of the country by proclaiming that throughout our nation's history, God placed "a hedge of protection around the United States." This hedge has protected us from war, famine, and pestilence, and we have earned this divine protection because of our "honest, God-fearing way of life."[52] Now, however, that protection can no longer be guaranteed. According to Robertson, immorality runs rampant; pornography, divorce, drug and alcohol addiction, abortion, and homosexuality have overrun the land. Clearly, the United States has rejected God and has declined to be a part of the holy beginnings of our nation's history. Instead, claims Robertson, we prefer to fortify our country on "decadence, deception and violence." Any protection that America has hitherto received will be removed—except perhaps certain groups that have been fasting and praying.[53] The religious right has an urgency about its mission and believes that the continued existence of the country is at stake, as is the salvation of millions upon millions of souls.

The debilitated condition of the contemporary family is central to what must be fixed in order to assure the salvation of America. Spokespersons of the religious right connect the desperate straits facing the institution of the family with the possibility that our entire society is in "danger of total collapse." Far from embracing the changing shape of the family, the religious right is convinced that we are on "the brink of destruction" unless we return to the true way of Christian family life.[54] If the family could only be healed of its ills, then a whole host of problems would cease to trouble us. This conviction echoes a Victorian worldview, which posited that the building block of a moral nation was the Christian family and, furthermore, that the stability of the Christian family was directly related to the well-being, if not the survival, of the nation. In a sermon first published in 1949, Peter Marshall (the former chaplain of the U.S. Senate) echoed this sentiment:

> I think of women, and particularly of our mothers, as Keepers of the Springs. . . . There never has been a time when there was a greater need for Keepers of the Springs, or when there were more polluted springs to be cleansed. If the home fails, the country is doomed. The breakdown of home life and influence will mark the breakdown of the nation. If the Keepers of the Springs desert their posts or are unfaithful to their responsibilities, the future outlook of this country is black indeed.[55]

Then, as now, connections were made between the sanctity of home life and the very survival of the nation. The ideal of a morally upright Christian family holding the future of a Christian nation in its hands became part and parcel of the American Dream in the early part of the Victorian era as changes took place in gender roles and in family life in general. During this period of cultural change, women were a central part of the picture; any deviation from proscribed gender roles might result in a disastrous compromise of the well-being of the nation. Churches perpetuated the American Dream of the ideal Christian home and connected it with Christian citizenship. The values inherent in this connection provided a moral cornerstone for church teachings.[56]

This vision of a Christian America shared by the Christian family is a very large part of the ideal upheld by the religious right today. The son of Peter Marshall sees it as the duty of "every Bible-believing American" to enter the political fray on behalf of the family and fight in the "spiritual and moral civil war for the soul of America." Indeed, it is only by doing so, claims the junior of the Marshalls, that the nation stands any chance of avoiding God's curse.[57] As we turn next to examine the literature of particular groups in the religious right, it will become even more apparent that any change in family life is interpreted as a menace to the moral fabric of society and, thus, to the survival of the nation as a whole. The contemporary specters of violent crime, the rise in the number of unwed mothers, the downward spiral of the quality of public education, and so-called broken families are markers of the disturbing fact that, according to the religious right, "we are in a race between civilization and catastrophe." Religion—in particular, religion of the Christian right variety—is "on the side of civilization."[58] This, as we shall see in the next chapter, is the underpinning of the arguments for family values.

2

To Save the Family

The heart of family life is marriage, the key organizing principle
behind all civilization. . . . No other relationship provides society
what marriage does. No other relationship transforms young
men and women into more productive, less selfish and more
mature husbands and wives, and fathers and mothers, than
marriage. No other relationship affords children the best
economic, emotional and psychological environment. Only as
we have drifted from the defense of marriage have we experienced soaring social problems, such as divorce, illegitimacy,
sexually transmitted diseases, and crime. The answer is not to
push the envelope further but to restore the primacy of marriage
within the law and the culture.[1]

Robert Knight, Family Research Council

In his 1994 book, *Politically Incorrect*, Ralph Reed brashly declared
that what the religious right really wants "is to make the restoration of the two-parent, intact family with children the central and
paramount public policy priority of the nation."[2] Quoting Alexis
de Tocqueville, Reed recalled the "peaceful society" that had once
existed in the family: "When the American retires from the turmoil of public life to the bosom of his family, he finds in it the
image of order and peace." According to Reed, restoring that peace
and order to family life is, ultimately, what will restore civility to
society as a whole and salvation to the country.[3]

All of the varied organizations that make up the amorphous
movement known as the religious right concur that the family is
the most critical of all social institutions. Indeed, the well-being
of the traditional family is the raison d'être of their political ac-

tivity. Any threat to the traditional family, no matter how seemingly trivial and no matter how clueless others may be about a particular perceived threat, is seen as tearing apart the American family. Furthermore, these threats are understood to pose grave danger to the moral fabric of the entire nation and, if left unchecked, will bring about the collapse of the family and the decline of civilization itself. Such threats, the religious right has surmised, must be quickly countered and soundly defeated.

The fate of the traditional family is always entwined with that of the entire social order. Jerry Falwell maintains that the "continued health" of the institution of the family "is a prerequisite for a healthy and prosperous nation."[4] Without the continued health of the traditional family, rates of "crime, poverty, academic failure, and personal unhappiness" will continue to rise.[5] Ralph Reed, the former head of the Christian Coalition, notes that most conservative Christians are, by nature, reluctant to become politically involved. Their only justification for entering into the political fray is the belief that the values they hold dearest are threatened. "The culture, the family, a loss of values, a decline in civility, and the destruction of our children" motivate them to political action.[6] The result: the family becomes the primary focus of public policy strategy and the battleground upon which the ensuing culture war is waged.

THE PLAYERS

Even though the various groups that make up the religious right agree on the need to defend the institution of the family as the overarching issue, we must remember that the religious right is not a monolithic movement. Far from it! This movement is made up of a variety of groups, whose foci cover a broad array of concerns. The groups differ in terms of their approaches, their political strategies, and their sense of which critical aspect of the threat to the institution of the family deserves immediate attention. Describing some of the key organizations may be helpful before delving much deeper into the content of their arguments. By so doing, a more detailed context in which the arguments are formulated and a deeper understanding of how the arguments come together as a whole to influence the wider social order emerges. The following pages examine the Christian Coalition (CC); the Christian Broadcasting Network (CBN); the American Family Association (AFA); the Promise Keepers (PK); Concerned Women for America (CWA); the Institute on Religion and Democracy (IRD); the Ecumenical Coalition on Women and Society (ECWS); a variety of other Christian women's groups; Focus on the Family (FOF) and its political arm, the Family Research Council (FRC); the Traditional Values Coalition (TVC); and a few representative conservative groups within mainline denominations. These groups are certainly some of the main players on the field of the religious right; however, they by no means represent all of the existing groups. Suffice it to say that these organizations paint the canvas in broad strokes and give the uninitiated reader a context in which to place the arguments of the religious right.

The Christian Coalition

> We're going to have a pro-family, conservative sitting in the White House so help us God. . . . It will be a millennium fraught with peril. . . . I want to see victory where the conservatives control the House of Representatives, where they control the Senate of the United States, where they control the White House, where they control the bureaucracy, where they have made drastic changes across the United States, where we have the governors' mansions, where we have people all over who love this nation, who love families, and are willing to sacrifice in order to make this one day truly one nation under God.[7]

In 1989, in the aftermath of his presidential defeat, Pat Robertson founded the Christian Coalition—billed as "a grassroots citizens' organization"—to give "pro-family Christians" a voice in the democratic process.[8] Using a list of three million people who had signed his election petitions, Robertson already had a core basis upon which to found the Coalition. According to the Christian Coalition's own Internet Web site, the organization boasts a cadre of nearly two million activists and supporters in more than 2,000 Christian Coalition chapters across the nation and has a network of 60,000 churches that help to educate voters about political issues affecting families.

A 1994 survey, conducted by the organization's publication, *Christian American*, found that the denominational affiliation of the membership was as follows: 5 percent Catholic, 23 percent Baptist, 9 percent Assemblies of God, 10 percent Pentecostal, and 35 percent nondenominational. A total of 14 percent identified themselves as being from mainline Protestant churches (including Lutherans, Methodists, and Presbyterians). A survey in 1995 reported that 9 percent of all members did not finish high school, 56 percent have either a high school or a vocational school diploma, and 32 percent finished college and/or graduate school. Despite the organization's claims that African American communities are solidly behind it, African Americans make up a scant 3 percent of the membership.[9]

The 1995 survey also revealed that 68 percent of Coalition membership self-identified as Republican, 20 percent as Independents, and only 5 percent as Democrats, making the group's claim to nonpartisanship increasingly difficult for its critics to believe.[10] In an October 1998 fund-raising letter, Randy Tate, then executive director of the Christian Coalition, reiterated that the Christian Coalition is nonpartisan and is not affiliated with the Republican Party in any way. He defended this claim by noting how upset the Christian Coalition is with Republican leaders who are ignoring the moral issues facing the nation and added that the Coalition is eager "to join hands with members of any party who share our commitment to put moral values back into American public life and to insist on political leaders who desire to strengthen rather than undermine the traditional marriage-based family."[11] However, despite the Christian Coalition's protests to the contrary, at its 1998 Road to Victory Conference in Washington, D.C., one got the feeling that Democrats were distinctly unwelcome. The event was a two-day-long pep talk for the conservative Republican team, which championed the pro-family candidates in the election arena. Trent Lott, the Senate majority leader, received a standing ovation when he voiced his intention that the religious right would defeat four Democratic senators in upcoming November elections. He announced, "This is the year that we can nail down a solid pro-life, pro-family majority in the U.S. Senate." Similarly, Senator Mitch McConnell called for Republican victories in the fall elections, proclaiming that "we have the opportunity to change the direction of America this November."[12]

The Coalition's stated mission is organized around the following goals: (1) to represent Christian viewpoints before local, state, and national legislative bodies; (2) to proclaim Christian values in the secular context as well as in the media; (3) to equip leaders to engage in effective social and political action; (4) to educate Christians about legislative issues affecting them; and (5) to protest any display of anti-Christian prejudice.[13] Ralph Reed, the former head of the Christian Coalition, summed up these goals by vowing that the Christian Coalition would not rest until Christians are involved in the public arena in a manner that is in keeping with their vast numbers. He added, "Americans are hungry for change, common sense, and a return to traditional values."[14]

In keeping with its goals, the Coalition released in 1995 what it termed "a bold and mainstream agenda to strengthen families and restore common-sense values" (aptly entitled a "Contract with the American Family"). This contract followed previous efforts on behalf of the Contract with America, emphasizing welfare reform and tax relief for families. The goal of the "Contract with the American Family" was to force the government to respond to "the cultural crisis" afflicting the country.[15] Reed likened the contract to a blueprint for addressing the most urgent issues facing U.S. society: "the fraying of the social fabric, the coarsening of the culture, the breakup of the family, and the decline in civility."[16] The contract included such items as passing the Religious Freedom Amendment (also known as the Istook Amendment), which would have allowed prayer in schools and other public settings; doing away with the federal Department of Education and returning control of education to local school boards; passing legislation to allow parents to choose their children's schools; revising tax laws to favor traditional families; placing limits on late-term abortions while simultaneously eliminating funds to organizations that perform abortions; protecting children from pornography; eliminating federal funding of the National Endowment for the Arts and Humanities, the Corporation for Public Broadcasting, and the Legal Services Corporation; encouraging private charities instead of the government to care for needy persons; enacting a Parental Rights Act and defeating the United Nations Convention on the Rights of the Child; and building more prisons to keep society safer.[17]

After the disappointments wrought by the Reagan/Bush years, when it became clear that the agenda of the religious right would not be acted upon by even the friendliest of presidential administrations, the strategy of the Christian Coalition shifted from depending upon the goodwill of the White House to focusing on the grassroots approach: namely, "one family at a time, one church at a time, one neighborhood at a time, one community at a time."[18] The new strategy, elaborated upon in an article in the Heritage Foundation's *Policy Review*, recognized that limited success had been attained by zeroing in exclusively on the issues of abortion and homosexuality. To attain a wider appeal, their emphasis was broadened to attract the loyalties of more mainstream voters by focusing on such issues as taxes, health care, crime, and economics. The key to the plan: persuading people to hold the government accountable. Reed insisted that those who voted with the agenda of the religious right were motivated not by a punitive desire to legislate "against the sins of others," but by "devotion to their children" and the ever-present, all-consuming need to strengthen the family.[19]

In March 1998, the Christian Coalition held a summit with two dozen key leaders of the political and religious right to strategize ways to get the Republican Party to champion their issues more aggressively. Frustrated with political stonewalls, the participants conveyed the necessity of obtaining a serious commitment to their agenda from the GOP. Various leaders threatened to leave the Republican Party if their concerns were not addressed.

In the absence of any substantive forthcoming response, the Christian Coalition forged full speed ahead with a battle plan. The current strategy is to focus less on a national level and more on local and state levels. One goal is to recruit, coach, and support the next crop of local conservative candidates, especially pro-life women.[20] Early in 1998, the Christian Coalition announced its Families 2000 strategy, focused specifically on placing family issues on the front burner in the next two presidential elections and well into the next century. The Families 2000 strategy incorporates a list of family-centered issues for local and state action, including state bans on partial birth abortion; passage of state parental rights and notification laws (for example, so that the parents of any teenagers who sought birth control or abortion would be notified); promotion of the involvement of parents in educational issues, including the local control of education; repeal of lesbian/gay civil rights initiatives, and the defeat of state adoption laws allowing lesbian and gay people to adopt; the protection of children from pornography; legislation limiting the expansion of legalized gambling; the defeat of drug legalization laws; and state legislation promoting covenant marriage contracts. National legislative goals include overriding Clinton's veto of the partial birth abortion ban; education reform; family tax relief eliminating the marriage tax penalty; and passage of the Istook Amendment on religious freedom.[21]

The strategy of this new initiative is to inspire a movement grounded in the local church community. Families 2000 emphasizes grassroots activism in local churches and has set as a goal recruiting one hundred thousand "church liaisons" by November 2000. By focusing on churches as the base for grassroots organizing, the Coalition aims to solidify its supporters in both suburban and urban locales. Since church congregations invariably serve as the prime source of people interested in conservative political action, the Coalition expects this strategy to boost its membership rolls, strengthen its cause, and support its annual budget.[22]

Despite its claims to be growing, the Christian Coalition called an emergency meeting in March 1999 to restructure the organization. The Coalition's president, Don Hodel, resigned to go back into retirement—reportedly soon after Pat Robertson suggested that the Republicans should stop pursuing Clinton's impeachment trial. Ralph Reed had resigned from the organization's board in December 1998. In June of 1999, the IRS revoked the group's nonprofit, tax-exempt status. Robertson now heads the organization.[23]

THE CHRISTIAN BROADCASTING NETWORK

Pat Robertson established the Christian Broadcasting Network in 1960 as a shoestring operation. To keep the fledgling network afloat, he hosted a telethon, marketing the network as a club of 700 supporters who, if each gave ten dollars, would enable CBN to survive financially. The 700 Club, as the group of supporters soon became known, grew exponentially, as did the network. In 1966, Robertson added his own program to the broadcast lineup and dubbed it *The 700 Club* in honor of his early supporters. Today, *The 700 Club* claims a daily audience of more than one million viewers, airs in more than ninety countries, and is broadcast in forty-six languages.

Since then, the multifaceted Christian Broadcasting Network has grown to be one of the largest Christian television networks in existence; it includes several national and international broadcasting networks, a twenty-four-hour-a-day telephone prayer line, an international relief organization, a hotel and conference center complex, and Regent University, which offers graduate degrees in several fields.[24] Truly, the Christian Broadcasting Network is a prime example of the elaborate and sophisticated infrastructure developed by the religious right.

THE AMERICAN FAMILY ASSOCIATION

Originally founded in 1977 by a United Methodist minister, the Rev. Donald Wildmon, in Tupelo, Mississippi, as the National Federation for Decency, the American Family Association describes itself as an organization "for people who are tired of cursing the darkness and who are ready to light a candle."[25] Wildmon explains what led him to found the AFA: "One evening in 1977 I sat down with my family to watch TV. On one channel was adultery, on another cursing, on another a man beating another over the head with a hammer. I asked the children to turn off the TV. I sat there, got angry, and said, 'They're going to bring this into my home, and I'm going to do all I can do to change it.'"[26]

The organization advocates traditional family values and focuses primarily on protesting television programming showing excessive sex and violence, as well as programming thought to portray anti-Christian bigotry. In particular, the AFA has campaigned against the Public Broadcasting Service (PBS), most recently by objecting to the showing of *Tales of the City*; the AFA has called for reduced funding for, if not the total shutdown of, public broadcasting as well. With a well-organized direct mail and print advertising campaign, the AFA also led the protest against the National Endowment for the Arts (NEA) and has engaged in issues involving local public school censorship. President Donald Wildmon explained, "What we are up against is not dirty words and dirty pictures. It is a philosophy of life which seeks to remove the influence of Christians and Christianity from our society."[27]

The AFA does not like to be perceived as being hostile to any group and specifically refutes the charge of being hostile to homosexuals. While admitting that it rejects the "sin of homosexuality," the AFA insists that the mission of its members is to love their neighbors. Indeed, that love inspires them to "expose the misrepresentation of the radical homosexual agenda and stop its spread through our culture." The AFA is eager to reach out to those in the homosexual life and let them know of the love and healing available "at the Cross of Christ."[28] Similarly, the AFA claims that it does not advocate censorship, since it understands censorship to be something imposed by the government. However, AFA members consider themselves to be advocates of "responsibility" and thus encourage advertisers to support only what can be described as quality, traditional-family-friendly programming.[29]

The AFA claims to have between 1.7 and 1.8 million people on its membership rolls, yet a *Newsweek* article in 1995 placed that number significantly lower—at 400,000 members. With a budget of more than $10 million, a staff of 40 employees, 4 full-time lawyers, and 450 local chapters across the nation, the AFA is well positioned to organize campaigns against materials and programs found to be most objectionable. The *AFA Journal*, published monthly, has a circulation of nearly 500,000, and the thirty-minute radio program, the *AFA Report*, is broadcast over an estimated 1,200 radio stations. In addition, the AFA has its own radio station network—American Family Radio—and boasts more than 100 radio stations in 24 states.[30]

THE PROMISE KEEPERS

The Promise Keepers came onto the scene in March 1990 when Bill McCartney, head football coach at the University of Colorado, and Dave Wardell, a physical education professor at the same institution, were brainstorming about what they would do with their lives if money were no object. Both men responded that they would work with men on a one-to-one basis, helping them to grow stronger in their Christian faith. As the two shared their dreams, the idea of a new men's movement emerged, and soon McCartney gathered together a group of seventy men to pray about a Christian-focused men's movement. Within a short time, they held their first conference.

Like many similar organizations on the right, Promise Keepers emphasizes the need to stand strong against "the sliding sludge caused by the erosion of values in society."[31] Violence, racial tensions, compromised marriage vows, substance abuse, unwed mothers, rising divorce rates, and the many transgressions that fall under the rubric of sexual immorality signal to those who have joined Promise Keepers that, unless there is a movement to turn things around, society is headed toward inevitable destruction. In the context of a compromised social order, Promise Keepers offers to help men incorporate strong Christian values into their lives. PK president Randy Phillips noted, "Our focus is changing men's hearts. When they're changed, they change a family, and a family can change a nation."[32]

The organization defines itself as "a Christ-centered ministry," dedicated to bringing together men who will be "godly influences" in the world. In a time of slipshod values and confusion around men's roles and identities, Promise Keepers maintains that men must encounter the Word of God and involve themselves in relationships of depth with God, their families, and one another. Promise Keepers believes that God is using the organization "to ignite a nationwide movement calling men . . . to reconciliation, discipleship, and Godliness." This movement starts with each individual man developing a relationship with Jesus Christ.[33]

Promise Keepers promotes itself as a place where men can go to discuss the intimate issues of their lives among themselves. Men return home from the conferences with a plan to connect to a small group, where they discuss the confusing role of the modern man, admit their personal shortcomings, and receive Christ-centered guidance from their peers. This aspect of Promise Keepers has come under some criticism, with the main objection focused on whether or not the small peer groups exert too much control over men's lives.

Despite the group's self-identification as nonpartisan, its founder Bill McCartney has been associated with Colorado for Family Values in the fight against civil rights for lesbian and gay people, as well as with the fervently antiabortion activist group Operation Rescue. Promise Keepers also has close ties to such conservative figures as Pat Robertson, whose program *The 700 Club* has featured segments on Promise Keepers and interviews with Bill McCartney. James Dobson, head of Focus on the Family, helped fund Promise Keepers and provided staff from his organization to Promise Keepers in the early days. In addition, Focus on the Family's publishing house publishes some key Promise Keepers literature. Bill Bright, who founded the Campus Crusade for Christ, has graced the conference stage at Promise Keepers' events and is known for being a vocal opponent of homosexuality, abortion, and the teaching of evolution. And although Promise Keepers' speakers are routinely urged to avoid controversial issues when addressing conferences, inevitably, one will say something that the Promise Keepers' leaders would rather he had not. (For example, at the Los Angeles 1995 Conference, speaker E. V. Hill called the American Civil Liberties Union "satanic.")[34]

Other controversial aspects of Promise Keepers include concern over its call for male headship and female submission and its emphasis on racial reconciliation—not through integration, but through particular relationships. At rallies, white men are urged to make friends with men of color and embrace them, taking that moment to turn away from their racism.[35] Some argue that the men who go to Promise Keepers' events cannot be as easily categorized in terms of politics as can the organization's leadership and may not have a political agenda for the group, but a survey conducted by the *Washington Post*, during the October 1997 national rally in Washington, D.C., revealed that Promise Keepers are generally Republican in politics and conservative in orientation. Fifty-five percent of those in attendance voted for Republican candidate Bob Dole in the 1996 presidential election, while only 15 percent voted for Bill Clinton. Sixty percent categorized themselves as "conservative" or "very conservative" and said that they were favorably inclined toward the religious right. And even though the organization purports to be apolitical, more than 50 percent of those surveyed by the *Washington Post* believed that the Promise Keepers should take an official position against same-sex marriages, and 94 percent opposed allowing same-sex couples to marry. Sixty-nine percent agreed that divorces ought to be made more difficult to obtain.[36]

In 1996, Promise Keepers held an unprecedented Clergy Conference, attracting more than thirty-nine thousand male ministers (women clergy were not invited). Keen on developing a nationwide network, the organization is also branching out on an international level. Similar in some respects to the strategy of the Christian Coalition, Promise Keepers hopes to place in every church in the country a "key man" who will work directly with the (presumably male) pastor to coordinate small group programs for men. These key men report to "ambassadors" stationed across the nation, who in turn are accountable to the national leadership. In 1995, 13,842 men were working with Promise Keepers' state offices to develop further this elaborate infrastructure. In 1990, 72 men attended the first Promise Keepers gathering. The number of men attending such conferences peaked at 1.1 million in 1996 and was recorded at 453,000 in 1998.[37]

CONCERNED WOMEN FOR AMERICA

Founded in 1979 by Beverly LaHaye, this antigay, antireproductive rights, and antisex education organization is also against funding for the National Endowment for the Arts, is opposed to sex education materials that do not advocate abstinence as the only option, and has campaigned against gay/lesbian civil rights legislation in several states. Originally created to counter the National Organization for Women and the Equal Rights Amendment, CWA has a budget that has grown to $10 million. With more than 1,200 chapters across the nation, CWA boasted a membership of 600,000 (100,000 of which are male) in 1996 and counts itself as the largest pro-family organization for women. The organization publishes two monthly periodicals, and its daily radio show, entitled *Beverly*

LaHaye Live, reaches an estimated 750,000 people, covering topics such as the economy, the threat that secular humanism poses to the educational system, and advice for first-time mothers.

A recent broadcast of *Beverly LaHaye Live* put forward the proposition that wives and mothers, not men, are the target of radical feminism. This sentiment is much in keeping with LaHaye's original motivation for founding CWA: in 1979, LaHaye heard Betty Friedan, founder of the National Organization for Women, claim to speak for all women and took offense at the presumptuousness of that claim. She refuted Friedan and denounced feminism as a movement that demeaned women who valued their roles as wives and mothers. She founded CWA in order to "protect the interests of American families and provide a voice for women . . . who believe in Judeo-Christian values."[38] LaHaye has declared that she is "consumed" by the problem of homosexuality. "Of all the problems in America today," she believes that "the homosexual movement poses the most serious threat to families and children."[39]

Members of CWA involve themselves in all aspects of public policy from the national and state levels to town councils and local school boards. Its stated mission is to protect and advocate Scripture-based values among the U.S. citizenry through prayer, education, and political involvement with the hope that such actions will reverse the national decline of morality. From its headquarters in Washington, D.C., CWA considers itself to be well positioned to offer authoritative advice and updates on national legislative issues affecting the family.

The Institute on Religion and Democracy

The Washington-based Institute on Religion and Democracy (IRD) came into the public eye in 1983 when *60 Minutes* and *Reader's Digest* focused on the organization's attacks on both the World and the National Councils of Churches (the WCC and NCC were charged with being too sympathetic to communism). Created in early 1981, the IRD has focused heavily on international issues (especially on Central America in the eighties[40] and on South Africa, by seeking an alternative to the African National Congress) and helped to develop conservative groups within mainline denominations to support the IRD agenda.

With the ending of the cold war, the IRD revamped its priorities and, in 1993, latched onto and promoted the conservative backlash from the Re-Imagining Ecumenical Women's Conference.[41] Ultimately, "radical feminism" replaced the specter of communism as IRD's focus. More recently, the IRD has criticized the efforts of the NCC to raise funds for rebuilding burned African American churches, challenging the accuracy of the number of burned churches as well as the motivation of the NCC. The IRD maintains that the NCC exploited the issue as a way of blaming conservatives for racism.[42]

Diane Knippers, who became president of the organization in 1993, trumpeted success in her inaugural speech: "The once monolithic mainline is now universally acknowledged as the sideline. No longer can the pompous prophets of 475 Riverside Drive pretend to represent Christendom."[43] Well known as the headquarters for the NCC, WCC, and some denominations, 475 Riverside Drive is widely castigated in conservative Christian circles as the source of liberalism (or secular humanism, or communism, or feminism, depending on which issue is being hotly debated at the time), which pollutes the mainline churches. Knippers further stated that the direction of the IRD was to be focused increasingly on environmental theology and on countering the feminist theological movement. More overarching domestic issues such as the teaching of moral values, church-state issues, and educational issues are high on the agenda. Threats to American decency that the organization has vowed to fend off include "extreme individualism; demands for 'rights' over 'responsibilities'; expecting the state rather than a range of social institutions to satisfy demands; and cultivating ethnic and gender differences in ways that alienate."[44]

THE ECUMENICAL COALITION ON WOMEN AND SOCIETY

The Institute on Religion and Democracy sired a group known as the Ecumenical Coalition on Women and Society (ECWS). This politically sophisticated group's stated intent is to counter feminist theology and, in particular, to counter the Re-Imagining movement. While championing the renewal movement within the nation's churches in general, the ECWS focuses primarily on countering the work "of radical feminists who argue that Christian teachings were first 'imagined' by men and now should be 'reimagined' by women." The threefold pledge of action is to (1) "reverse detrimental cultural trends," (2) "expose the assumptions at the foundation of the radical feminists' philosophy," and (3) press for a renewal of biblical orthodoxy in the church and for a more central role for faith in society.[45] One of its enthusiastic supporters notes, "Working for preservation of the traditional Christian Faith, in the face of radical feminism and other current movements advocating its 're-imagining' or reconstruction, constitutes the most effective action that can be undertaken today for the welfare of humanity."[46]

The ECWS maintains that religious feminists are undermining the churches and declares that the recent trend in feminist theology to incorporate multicultural and interreligious themes in worship experiences is idolatrous. Alarmed at the feminist corpus of liturgies that has grown up in the last few years, the ECWS denounces what it terms "radical feminist rituals and songs that focus on women's suffering and victimization and obsessively glorify women's bodies and sexuality." Furthermore, the group objects to the feminist theological (and that of other liberation theologies) epistemological privileging of human experience and criticizes the structural analysis of racism, classism, and sexism, preferring instead to focus on the individual need for repentance and Christian conversion. The ECWS is troubled also by the feminist focus on women's professional participation in the church, feeling that too much emphasis is placed on deployment quotas.[47]

The ECWS claims that the feminist agenda is a revolutionary one that seeks to restructure society. Specifically, the organization rejects social construction theory as a lens through which to interpret gender and, instead, insists that human sexuality is firmly ensconced in the biological categories of male and female. The members also claim that the suffering of women has been exaggerated and that women have been overly portrayed as victims of male abuse and oppression. Last, but not least, the ECWS is concerned about the same issues that capture the attention of many of its sister organizations on the religious right: no-fault divorces, abortion, and lesbianism. Members firmly repudiate any "tolerance for sinful behavior patterns," believing that these behavior patterns are based on the false assumption that pleasure is what creates human fulfillment and that, as such, should be the primary goal of life.[48] The ECWS fervently objects to what it terms "the glorification of sexual lifestyles without limits or consequences and views of marriage and family that contradict biblically-based faith and time-tested moral behavior."[49]

The Re-Imagining Conference clearly pushed buttons among those on the religious right to the extent that an entire organization was formed to counter it. The conference served as a wake-up call to the religious right—and particularly to conservative groups within mainline denominations—and brought a great deal of attention to bear on the corpus of feminist theological work that had developed since the late 1960s. Political commentator Charmaine Crouse Yoest put it this way: "Feminism no [longer] stands on uncontested ground." Feminist theologians should be "on notice that we intend to fight back on behalf of the next generation of women. We need not reimagine our faith. We need only boldly declare it."[50]

OTHER CHRISTIAN WOMEN'S GROUPS

Increasing numbers of groups for women have evolved in recent years. Several women's groups have arisen from the Promise Keepers men's movement with such names as Aspiring Women, Time Out, Suitable Helpers (which believes that women need "counseling" in order to accept their zealous Promise Keepers husbands), Chosen Women, Renewing the Heart, Promise Reapers (which holds the position that women were "born from the side of Promise Keepers, as Eve was from Adam's side"), Women of Faith, and Heritage Keepers (which teaches women to "let go of the reins" of family control when an enthusiastic husband returns from a Promise Keepers rally and advocates female submission as an honor).[51] These groups, which are growing slowly but steadily, hold conferences to help women become stronger Christians and better helpmates to their men. While Promise Keepers has only male speakers at its stadium events, the women's groups have both men and women speakers to avoid seeming "feminist."[52] One young woman at a Chosen Women rally described a woman's job as being "to submit to our teachers and our Professors . . . even if we know they are wrong. It is then in God's hands."[53]

Jill Briscoe, a prominent figure in evangelical women's circles, maintains that being concerned about sexism is a luxury. She explains, "As long as we can agree on the fundamentals like salvation, heaven, hell, Jesus Christ, then where women fit in the church hierarchy will have to wait."[54] Bunny Wilson, the author of *Liberation Through Submission*, argues that women's attention should be focused completely on the family and, furthermore, that they should refrain from competing with men. Women, Wilson insists, need to focus on the unique feminine characteristics of sensitivity, mothering, compassion, and intuition in order to build up the family rather than taking over the man's leadership role.[55]

Women for Faith and Family is a Roman Catholic group formed to support the traditional teachings of the church and the authority of the pope. The women not only oppose the movement for the ordination of women, but they also feel that girls should not serve as acolytes, that women should not be allowed to give homilies, and that inclusive-language scriptural translations, liturgies, hymns, and homilies undermine the authority of the church. These women are concerned as well about the destructive effect of feminism on the church, on the traditional family, and on society in general, and they believe that women should not appropriate so-called male characteristics that might counter their own femininity.[56]

Renew, the women's program group of the United Methodist conservative group, Good News, works to bring its point of view to the more liberal organization, United Methodist Women (UMW). At the 1998 annual UMW Assembly, Renew presented its perspectives on homosexuality, radical feminism, abortion, and spiritual renewal. The primary agenda is to counter "radical feminist theology" (especially that espoused by Re-Imagining), which denies scriptural authority, questions the necessity of the atonement while emphasizing the corporate (rather than personal) nature of sin, and asserts that all religions lead to God. In response to the criticism that Renew was too narrow, spokeswoman Faye Short responded, "We get that attitude from One who said, '. . . small is the gate and narrow the road that leads to life . . . ,' and, 'I am the way and the truth and the life. No one comes to the Father except through me.' May we never be bold enough to broaden that perspective."[57]

Women in movements such as Renew firmly believe in holding to narrow definitions of what it means to be Christian and what constitutes Christian behavior. They feel that attempting to broaden that perspective is viewed as heresy and, ultimately, poses a threat to family, society, and church.

Focus on the Family

James Dobson, a psychologist and the host of a popular Christian radio program, has long been concerned about the health of the American family. In 1977, he founded Focus on the Family (FOF), beginning the ministry with a twenty-five-minute, weekly radio program. The organization has since grown to become international in scope with more than 74 ministries, 1,300 employees, 30 state chapters, 3.5 million people on the mailing list, 10 monthly periodicals, and a daily radio program broadcast to more than 4,000 stations throughout the world. Housed on a 47-acre complex in Colorado Springs, with an annual budget of $110 million, FOF is one of the larger organizations of the religious right. Like other groups, Focus on the Family organizes its work around a broad spectrum of family value issues, but has been especially hard-nosed on abortion (Dobson is a supporter of the militant anti-abortion group, Operation Rescue) and issues affecting lesbian/gay people. In August 1995, Dobson wrote an eight-page newsletter attacking the United Nations' women's conference in Beijing (which took place from August 30 to September 15, 1995). He described the conference as "the most radical, atheistic and antifamily crusade in the history of the world . . . [whose] goal is to give members of the human family five genders from which to choose. A person can decide whether to be male, female, homosexual, lesbian or transgendered. Some may want to try all five."[58] Focus on the Family facilitates workshops across the nation with the express purpose of educating conservative Christians on how to become involved in the political process.

The official ministries of FOF are diverse and include eleven different radio programs; fifteen publications; films, videos, and television programs; "personal touch ministries," which include outreach to lawyers, African American pastors, employees of corporate America, those in crisis because of pregnancy, chaplains, and physicians; the Institute for Family Studies; Dobson's syndicated newspaper column; seminars, workshops, and conferences; pro-family newspaper advertisements dealing with such issues as abortion, violence, sex, the dangers of condom use, and most recently, homosexuality; as well as international outreach in more than seventy countries.

FOF's primary purpose is to spread the gospel and, while doing so, to underscore the importance of the family. The five guiding, biblically focused "pillars" on which the mission is based are these: (1) the purpose of living is to know and glorify God, attaining eternal life through Jesus, beginning within one's own family and then moving outward to a fallen humanity unaware of the love of Jesus; (2) God meant marriage to be "a permanent, lifelong relationship between a man and a woman"; (3) children are a blessed inheritance from God, and we are responsible for preparing them for a life of Christian servanthood; (4) human life is priceless and to be valued at all times, from the unborn child to the moments before death comes; and (5) the family, as one of the three basic institutions that God has ordained, "exists to propagate the race and to provide a safe and secure haven in which to nurture, teach and love the younger generation."[59] These values, claims FOF, are rooted in Scripture and the Judeo-Christian heritage rather than being drawn from humanistic notions. Thus, these principles are from "the recommendations of the Creator Himself."

In 1984, Dobson was asked to join others concerned about the problems facing the family in a meeting with then President Ronald Reagan. Dobson made five recommendations about how government might be more responsive to the concerns of families. The first was that the president himself continue to provide "strong moral leadership with regard to traditional family values." Increased government support for the economic survival of marriage and parenthood constituted the second. The third involved the fact that under the rubric of the family, the institution of the family has no standing in U.S. constitutional law.[60] Dobson recommended that this issue be addressed, perhaps even by constitutional amendment. The funding with federal tax moneys of advocacy groups that Dobson considered to have antifamily positions (such as Planned Parenthood, Gay Partners, and NOW's Legal Defense Fund, among others) was the fourth issue Dobson highlighted. Cutting off the funding of such organizations was imperative. Dobson's last recommendation called for a review of "all agencies of the federal government to assess their impact on the institution of the family."[61] This last recommendation was acted upon in 1985, when Reagan asked Gary Bauer, then the undersecretary of the Department of Education (soon to become the senior domestic policy adviser for Reagan), to undertake a yearlong analysis of how the government affected families. Twelve years later, however, Dobson lamented the death of the policy, noting that President Clinton had effectively done away with the last part of Reagan's attempt to protect the family.

THE FAMILY RESEARCH COUNCIL

Originally founded in 1981, the Family Research Council (FRC) merged with James Dobson's Focus on the Family from 1988 to 1992, reorganizing separately in the fall of 1992, apparently for legal reasons so that the FRC might lobby more freely. Headed by Gary Bauer until he stepped down in 1999 to run for President, FRC is commonly regarded as the political arm of Focus on the Family. Dobson often refers to the two groups as "legally separate but spiritually one."[62] The FRC has a reputation as a conservative think tank, which aggressively organizes against reproductive rights, lesbian/gay civil rights, and funding for the National Endowment for the Arts and the Corporation for Public Broadcasting; in addition, the FRC seeks to reestablish school prayer and "disestablish" the Department of Education.[63] Claiming a membership of 250,000 supporters, the FRC publishes *Washington Watch*, a monthly periodical, and *Family Policy*, a bimonthly publication, and participates in the *Family News in Focus* radio broadcasts. Recently, the FRC formed a new political action committee called the Campaign for Working Families, which expressly targets the gay rights movement.

The organization's sole purpose is to "reaffirm and promote nationally, and particularly in Washington, DC, the traditional family unit and the Judeo-Christian value system upon which it is built."[64] To attain its purpose, the FRC has pledged to defend and promote traditional family values in the media, develop and advocate legislation and public policies that strengthen the family and promote traditional values, maintain a database that highlights the importance of the family to Western civilization, and educate the citizenry in terms of how biblical principles can best be promoted in contemporary culture.[65]

THE TRADITIONAL VALUES COALITION

Founded in 1981 by the Rev. Louis Sheldon, the Traditional Values Coalition (TVC) is best known for its antigay activities. This group, with a membership of 7,800 churches in California and a total of 31,000 churches (representing 12 denominations) across the nation, 20 state chapters, and an office in Washington, D.C., is relatively small in comparison to some of the other organizations of the religious right. Because of its size, the TVC must make the most of its $2 million annual budget. It focuses specifically on issues affecting education and works to oppose gay rights, reproductive freedom, the teaching of evolution in schools, and sex education that does not focus exclusively on abstinence. The group was central in persuading the California State Board of Education to reject a sex education curriculum that covered the subjects of homosexuality and AIDS, engaged in the Colorado and Oregon battles to outlaw civil rights protections for gay men and lesbians, and recently worked with groups in California, Arizona, Missouri, and Washington to organize antigay initiatives.[66]

Conservative Groups in Mainline Denominations

The Southern Baptist Convention (SBC) has been quite active lately in garnering support to oppose what is believed to be offensive to Christian sensibilities. The best-known campaign of late has focused on a boycott of Walt Disney Corporation because of the corporation's support of gay and lesbian people. The SBC annual convention in the summer of 1998 marked a significant historical moment in the denomination. The assembly not only chose to release a public statement regarding its stand on family values, but also chose to adopt that stand into its credo, the Baptist Faith and Message (which focuses primarily on the theological interpretation of sin, salvation, and spiritual growth). This action represents the first time in thirty-five years that the denomination has amended the document; not even the Great Depression, World War II, the Vietnam War, or the struggle for civil rights inspired such a move. Only rarely has the document touched on social issues. Clearly, the debate over family values has touched a deep nerve in the denomination.

Southern Baptist conservatives won the battle for control of the denomination in the 1980s (a battle that its critics call a "fundamentalist takeover" and that Jerry Falwell calls a "spiritual revolution")[67] and successfully shifted away from the ordination of women and other issues concerning women's leadership. As a result, they experienced an almost total turnover of faculty in their seminaries. The Southern Baptists' current stand on gender roles is much in line with that voiced by such organizations as the Family Research Council and the Promise Keepers. Indeed, the declaration regarding the necessity of wives to submit to their husbands takes several steps beyond the ambiguity commonly voiced by other groups of the religious right.

An article in the *Christian Century* notes that what the Southern Baptists mean by "submission" does not necessarily entail "blind obedience" to husbandly authority as much as it suggests "pliant cooperation and acceptance of familial obligations." The point of wifely submission is generally to consult one's husband regarding issues that affect the family. The authors further speculate that the doctrine of wifely submission is more about "male fantasies of power (and female collusion in such fantasies) than about most domestic realities."[68] The current enthusiasm regarding wifely submission seems to be rooted in the nostalgic longing for the harmonious sanctuary of the home in which the contemporary pressures of marital discord, economic stress, irresponsible men, and feminist unrest do not hold sway. The denomination overwhelmingly rejected amendments that would have required husbands and wives to submit to each other and one that would have included widows, widowers, and single persons under the rubric of "family."

The Good News Renewal movement of the United Methodist Church was launched in 1967 to express the deep consternation that many conservatives felt over the perception that their denomination had departed from biblical Christianity and the historic theological inheritance of John Wesley. The purpose of the more recently founded Confessing movement was to reaffirm traditional theology in the wake of the United Methodist Church's abandonment of the gospel. The ultimate issue for the Confessing movement is to make certain that the denomination still affirms Jesus Christ as "Son, Savior and Lord." In such a context, "the homosexuality challenge" is a central concern, and pressure is exerted on the denominational authorities to defend publicly the guiding principles of biblically based faith and moral absolutes. To fail to do so leaves the church open to criticism that members are merely professing Christ, not confessing Christ, and thus are inviting the devil to make headway in the church and world.[69]

Like members of other groups that locate themselves on the religious right, those in the United Methodist Church cite the "massive destruction of morality, honesty, safety, families, marriages, trust, the sanctity of life, sex, and even belief in objective truth and goodness" as the motivating factors for their activism in denominational circles.[70] Such issues, which are decidedly moral and theological in character, loom large on their horizon.

The Presbyterian Lay Committee was founded more than thirty years ago by those who believed that the tradition was being undermined by a new social agenda, as evidenced in the words: "The Scriptures are nevertheless the words of men." Those words were part of the 1967 Confession, which was approved by the denomination's legislative body (the General Assembly) and included in the denomination's Book of Confessions. The Lay Committee was founded out of the alarming possibility that the denomination might reduce Scripture to the status of human literature. When denominational officials refused to publish articles expressing those concerns, the Lay Committee paid for full-page advertisements in such publications as the *Wall Street Journal*, the *New York Times*, and the *Washington Post*. The first committee members predicted a large loss of membership in the denomination, a lack of emphasis on evangelism and mission, and what they termed "an invasive biblical illiteracy."[71] Currently, the Lay Committee works closely with sixteen other renewal groups in the Presbyterian Church (USA) to restore fidelity to biblical faith.

Members of the Presbyterian Lay Committee refused to sit by and watch a mass exodus from the church. Believing that their Christian duty was to be faithful to their denomination, they decided to publish their own periodical—the *Presbyterian Layman*. As one of the largest religious newspapers in the country, it claims a mailing list of more than 583,000 households. The *Layman* was instrumental in rejecting a Human Sexuality Report supporting lesbian and gay lifestyles, helped approve an amendment establishing ordination standards as "fidelity in marriage between a man and a woman and chastity in singleness," rejected the "re-imagining" of God as Sophia as being unbiblical, and helped defeat Amendment A, which would have permitted lesbian and gay people to enter the ranks of the clergy.[72] Parker T. Williamson, the *Layman*'s editor, is motivated to do his work by the need he perceives to oppose anything and everything having to do with liberation theology. He claims success in that he sees the stream of liberation theology drying up to a slow trickle in the denomination.[73]

Episcopalians United, founded in 1987, is a conservative pressure group with more than thirty thousand members within the Episcopal Church. Its battles in 1997 included the following foci: (1) to tell the truth—alerting church members across the nation to what is going on in their denomination; (2) to shine the light—portraying a positive model for "what the Church can and must become"; and (3) to support the protest—by encouraging those standing strong against "the perversion of Scripture."[74] The overarching goal of the organization is to return the church to a reliance on Scripture as the sole authority and to the roots of a traditional, conservative Christianity, which is "faithful to Scripture, Tradition and the Lordship of Jesus Christ."[75]

The group opposes the ordinations of "practicing, unrepentant homosexuals," the blessing of same-gender unions, and the use of inclusive language in church liturgies. Charging that too many leaders in the Episcopal Church have succumbed to societal pressures by refusing to preserve traditional Christian values, Episcopalians United vows to restore the broken church by mobilizing concerned laity and clergy to change the church.

The organizations surveyed in this chapter are only a representative sampling of groups doing work on these concerns. To be sure, among these groups are several influential ones. We must keep in mind the extent to which these groups have the power to influence public policy and set the agenda for denominational politics. As is evidenced from their sophisticated infrastructure, these organizations possess the means and the influence to shape the terms of the debate. Not one of these organizations should be dismissed lightly.

A SURVEY OF RELIGIOUS RIGHT ACTIVISTS

In 1997, the Bliss Institute of the University of Akron, in cooperation with the Institute for First Amendment Studies, polled twelve hundred religious right activists, six hundred of whom responded. The results of that small survey give us some intriguing factors to consider: 62 percent of respondents were male, 97 percent were white, and 85 percent were married. Most had a college or postgraduate degree and earned at least $25,000 a year. Seventy-one percent of respondents described their religious tradition as "evangelical Protestant" and indicated that they had these beliefs: Satan is a real being (92 percent), Jesus is the only way to salvation (87 percent), and the world is getting increasingly worse (81 percent). Regarding their views of society, 99 percent agreed that moral decay has caused the country's problems, 96 percent believe that Christians should be active in politics to defend their values, 91 percent feel that God works through politics and elections, another 91 percent perceive that the United States has benefited when it obeyed God, 89 percent agree that clergy and their churches should involve themselves in politics, 61 percent maintain that capitalism is the only economic system compatible with Christianity, and 75 percent believe that if only enough people came to Christ, social problems would be resolved. On the other hand, only 40 percent agreed that ethnic, racial, and religious diversity should be encouraged; 31 percent believed that a person could be both liberal and Christian; and a mere 21 percent thought that diverse views on moral issues should be tolerated. Groups perceived as having too much influence in society included the news media (98 percent), feminists (93 percent), the Hollywood movie industry (92 percent), atheists and agnostics (62 percent), and African Americans (46 percent). Ninety-six percent of religious right activists placed themselves somewhere on the conservative continuum, and 90 percent described themselves as a "leaning Republican," a "Republican," or a "strong Republican." Ninety percent voted for Bob Dole in the 1996 presidential election, with 28 percent indicating that Pat Buchanan was their first choice for the 1996 Republican Party presidential nomination.

Not surprisingly, 95 percent felt that abortion should be completely outlawed, except in circumstances where it was necessary to save the life of the mother. Ninety-three percent agreed that vouchers and tax credits should be made available so that parents are able to exercise some control over their children's schooling. Only 25 percent agreed that the federal government should be responsible for dealing with the problems of poverty. When queried about what groups needed more protection of their civil rights, 93 percent insisted that the traditional family needed more protection, 78 percent believed that religious people in general needed more protection, 56 percent thought that those who chose to school their children at home needed additional protection, and 42 percent felt that the rights of gun owners should be more protected. Only 11 percent of respondents indicated that African Americans needed more protection, and 9 percent that immigrants should be protected more. Predictably, 87 percent believed that the rights of lesbian women and gay men should be less protected.[76]

With some knowledge of the origins, strategies, and makeup of these organizations, we can turn now to the discussion of the threats they face. These threats are, they perceive, attacks against the family. Members of the religious right understand their God-ordained mission to be to defend the family, society as a whole, and the entire nation from these threats. For each threat, there is an answer. This discussion makes up the heart of the matter.

3

Threatened by Chaos,
Saved by Tradition

I . . . believe that when a nation violates the natural order of
things, it pays a terrible price. For example, the Judeo-Christian
tradition . . . [teaches] that sexual promiscuity is wrong and that
sex should be enjoyed only within the marriage covenant. But
now American elites reject that view, as do many ordinary
citizens, and as a result, modern American life is littered with the
broken bodies and abandoned women and children of the
sexual revolution. In each case where we have abandoned the
"natural law," we have suffered greatly.[1]

Gary Bauer

This chapter lays open the heart of the arguments of the religious
right. Two sorts of arguments can be distinguished: first, perceived
threats to the sanctity of family life; and second, solutions proposed to save the day. The surprise is not so much in the details
behind the positions as in their mainstream acceptance.

THREATS

That the religious right believes that the nation is facing a multi-
tude of threats is clear. Unlike other times in history, the threats,
they believe, come from within the nation's borders. According
to the religious right, in these perilous times in which we live,
families rapidly disintegrate, children are regularly abandoned,
abortion is performed more frequently than any other medical
procedure, and schools are unsafe environments for children. In
addition, society is haunted by the specters of illegitimacy, drug
addiction, homosexuality, street violence, and a high divorce rate.

All of these are considered to be threats to the well-being of the institution of the family. Add to this dire picture the debate around who constitutes a family, and it looks gloomy indeed to the religious right. The religious right is accusing the "liberal elites" of redefining the family outside the traditional model of husband, wife, and children. Since the traditional family is the only model of family that the pro-family movement considers valid and God ordained, this occasions a call to shore up the defenses against the oncoming siege and defend the sanctity of the family. In what follows, some of the more contemporary threats that the religious right has identified are explored in terms of how various aspects of the pro-family movement understand them.

THE HOMOSEXUAL AGENDA

James Dobson wrote,

> Why are we so concerned about the bias toward the homosexual agenda in the United States? Because it has profound implications for the well-being of our society. Any change in the traditional understanding of the family will undermine its legal foundation and render it meaningless. If, for example, marriage can occur between two men and two women, why not three men or four women? What about between siblings, or between parents and children? How about one man and six women, which reopens the polygamy debate of 116 years ago? To change the definition of marriage from the exclusive union between one man and one woman is to destroy the family as it has been known for 5,000 years.[2]

Lesbian women and gay men are the focus of a great deal of the religious right's vitriolic rhetoric. Homosexuality has been described as anathema, perverse, and "an abomination against Almighty God."[3] In June of 1998, Senate Majority Leader Trent Lott publicly stated that he believed that homosexuality was a sin, and Alan Keyes referred to "the radical homosexual agenda that assaults every idea of family responsibility."[4] Carmen Pate of Concerned Women for America asserts that "the homosexual lifestyle is about disease."[5]

National Football League player Reggie White, in speaking against civil rights for gay and lesbian people, declared that homosexual orientation is a choice and therefore is not an immutable characteristic worthy of civil rights legislation. He added, that while people from all ethnic backgrounds may identify as gay or lesbian, "people from all different ethnic backgrounds also are liars and cheaters and malicious and back-stabbers."[6] In response to Gay Day at Disney World, Pat Robertson warned Orlando, Florida, that it would be risking "some serious hurricanes" if it continued to welcome gay and lesbian people. Such toleration of homosexuality, proclaimed Robertson, would "bring about terrorist bombs. It [would] bring earthquakes, tornadoes, and possibly a meteor."[7] Robertson later claimed, in an effort to defend himself, that he had merely said,

> If you're going to have one month dedicated to waving the flag of the homosexuals, it isn't a very wise thing with the hurricane season coming up to wave a flag under God's nose.... We are a target. We have been a target. . . . If we continue to engage in various types of sexual conduct which is displeasing to God, then this country will not have the defenses we've enjoyed for such a long time. I said it then. I say it now. But I did not make those extreme comments.[8]

In that same month, the Southern Baptist Convention passed a resolution claiming that homosexuality is against biblical standards and is thus immoral; furthermore, any "open affirmation of homosexuality represents a sign of God's surrendering a society to its perversion."[9] Like Reggie White, the Southern Baptists also understand the world of "homosexual politics" to be appropriating the cause of the civil rights movement and insist that homosexual behavior and "other learned sexual deviance" have nothing in common with moral exhortations to stop discriminating on the basis of race and gender.[10]

The argument of the religious right is based on the premise that anyone who is homosexual in orientation can change. The alleged misinformation that those who are homosexual cannot change has convinced too many Americans, under false pretenses, to support lesbian and gay initiatives for civil rights. They argue that it is un-Christian to tell lesbian and gay people that there is no hope of change; such rhetoric, they claim, is tantamount to giving people the message that, therefore, they might as well take part in "sexual behavior that is unhealthy, immoral, and, in many cases, even fatal."[11] Furthermore, they maintain that, while it is not wrong to have homosexual desires, it is wrong to pursue those desires when they might be dangerous to oneself or to others. Homosexuality is discouraged, claims Robert Knight from the Family Research Council, not because anyone is homophobic, but because such behavior "hurts people, families, and communities."[12]

James Dobson, founder of Focus on the Family, laid out the right's position on homosexuality in his June 1998 newsletter. The two primary obstacles to building "bridges of understanding" to the gay community are based, he explained, on differing assumptions. The first obstacle Dobson cited was that there was no way around the fact that the Bible declares homosexual behavior to be sinful. Citing the Genesis account of creation, Dobson maintained that the passage provided a foundation on which all prohibitions of homosexuality were based and that therefore the practice of homosexuality was not only to be considered "morally equivalent" to heterosexual promiscuity, bestiality, and pedophilia, but "contrary to God's plan for the human family" as well.[13]

The second obstacle noted by Dobson was the fact that organizations such as Focus on the Family necessarily had to oppose the agenda of gay activists. Dobson declared that "their ideas are dangerous to society at large and to the family in particular." Unfortunately, to his consternation, advocates of the gay agenda seemed to be everywhere and had the potential to wreak "havoc on American culture."[14]

The religious right holds that homosexuality is a disorder, often comparable to alcoholism (or, as in Senator Trent Lott's remarks in the summer of 1998, to kleptomania), that can be cured. It is seen as a stunting of psychological and sexual growth, which should be treated as an addiction.[15] Claims that homosexuality is a curable condition were evident in the series of ads run during the summer of 1998 in *USA Today*, the *Washington Post*, and the *New York Times*. The catalyst behind the advertising campaign was Anthony Falzarano, president of the Washington-based Parents and Friends of Ex-Gays, who himself experienced liberation from the homosexual lifestyle, along with a coalition of fifteen pro-family organizations. The goal of the ads, asserts Falzarano, is to counter the lesbian/gay movement's assertion that sexual orientation is an immutable characteristic and to let people in the United States know that there is a strong ex-gay movement. These ads, written, so its authors believed, in the language of love and compassion, claimed that homosexuals could lead happy, fulfilled lives as heterosexuals if only they would admit that homosexual behavior was a sin and turn their lives over to Christ.[16] At the same time that the ad was run, the Family Research Council distributed a Capitol Hill Briefing Report that likened lesbian women and gay men to "an army of termites, secretly eating away the floorboards of the moral integrity in this country." Falzarano, to whom that quote is attributed, declared that it was time to expose the gay activist agenda for what it was—evil.[17] He added even more fuel to the controversy when he proclaimed on a Concerned Women for America radio program that "Satan uses homosexuals as pawns."[18] Falzarano urged that the United States refrain from legally recognizing the homosexual lifestyle since such recognition would not help homosexuals; it would only perpetuate a myth and deliver "them over to a deathstyle."[19]

The bottom line is that members of the religious right passionately believe that homosexuality is not part of God's design and, furthermore, that homosexuality is a sin on par with adultery and incest. The general sense is that homosexuals, by definition, represent a threat to children; their refusal to fit into the confines of the traditional family structure can be interpreted only as such. Clearly, only heterosexual activity within monogamous marriage is acceptable. Therefore, any legislation that might be interpreted as encouraging homosexual conduct is unacceptable. The sentiment of "love the sinner, hate the sin" is the most generous of the positions on the religious right. This sentiment is justified by the comparison of lesbian and gay people to teenage mothers: love and support are given to those teens, but premarital sex among young people (or any people for that matter) is not condoned.[20] Jerry Falwell's position is much less generous: he contends that

AIDS and other sexually transmitted diseases are evidence that God's wrath is being visited upon the whole society because of the sinners who have sex outside traditional marriage.[21]

"The homosexual agenda" is seen by those on the religious right as a master plan to destroy the traditional family and is understood to be wending its way into "Ourtown, USA." As evidence, the fact that homosexuals are no longer confined to the arts, but are part of many other professions is cited. To make matters worse, some liberal factions of mainline denominations have even declared that biblical prohibitions against same-sex relationships were merely cultural and therefore hold no moral weight.[22] This situation sets the scene for those who are part of the pro-family movement to interpret homosexuality as an encroaching threat upon life as they know it.

As the very existence of homosexuality challenges notions of family, so does the debate over extending work-related benefits to gay or lesbian couples in the same manner that they are extended to married heterosexual couples. Many fear that domestic partner benefits are part of the plan to blur the distinction between same-gender and heterosexual married couples. The granting of such benefits, opponents argue, presumes that domestic partnerships are equivalent to traditional marriages. Such a presumption, they argue, threatens the sanctity of the institution of marriage.[23]

In a similar vein, same-gender marriage is understood to be an attack against the essence of marriage. The acceptance of the former would deliver a serious blow to the already weakened institution of the family. Any government sanctioning of same-gender marriages would cause negative repercussions to the traditional family since government endorsement of various practices inevitably would cause those practices to become pervasive throughout the entire social order. In such a scenario, not only would the definition of marriage change, but the way would be paved for gay men and lesbian women to adopt children and become foster parents. In addition, school curricula would change to reflect new understandings of marriage and family; thus, children would be "indoctrinated" into seeing homosexuality as a lifestyle that is as valid as heterosexuality.[24] Those on the religious

right fear that if the "one man plus one woman" equation of traditional marriage is challenged, then there will be no limits placed
on marriage; they reason that if two men can marry or two women
can marry, then why not allow three people to marry, "or two adults
and a child, or consenting blood relatives of legal age?"[25] The Hawaii chapter of the Christian Coalition warned if same-gender
marriages are permitted to take place, then the "institution of marriage, as we know it, created by God, will come to an end throughout the world in six months to one year!"[26]

Many organizations on the religious right are increasingly re-
lying on this argument against the lesbian/gay movement for social change: any change would violate the religious beliefs of those
who oppose homosexuality by forcing homosexuality upon them
and would contribute to the ongoing deterioration of the social
order.[27] Perhaps Jack Elwood, pastor at Immanuel Bible Church
in Springfield, Virginia, captured the gist of the threat best when
he commented, "Homosexuality is not only an issue of morality,
but it is spilling over into public policy. It's in the court system. It's
in the political process. It's one of the things that is reflective of
our current culture."[28] And it can no longer be contained.

The Feminist Agenda

Alongside homosexuality, one of the greatest dangers to the Christian family is feminism. Beverly LaHaye describes feminism as
being "based on selfishness, rebellion, and anger" and claims it is
attempting to herald the destruction of an entire civilization.[29]
Feminists are perceived as one of the biggest threats to the traditional family because, in recent years, they have questioned nearly
every aspect of man-woman relationships, raising the proposition that the differences between the sexes are only culturally constructed. Many on the religious right believe that feminism came
into being because particular women were hurt and were unable
to forgive those who had hurt them. They view feminist ideology
as destructive and claim that it is responsible for holding the nation captive. This infestation of feminism has even become apparent in Christian homes where increasing numbers of women
are questioning the principle of subjection to male leadership.

James Dobson blames feminism for creating a "severe crisis of identity" for the American male; the result has been that male headship has been criticized and belittled. Feminism, he claims, has created confusion over gender roles and sexual identity and is deliberately attempting to "discredit the traditional role of manliness" by seeking "revolution within the family."[30] In an attempt to illustrate the futility of feminist efforts, Dobson admits that uncertainty regarding how a man should behave is running rampant throughout society and raises (for him) the ridiculous questions about how men and women should behave in particular situations:

> Is he a breadwinner and a protector of his family? Well, not exactly. Should he assume a position of leadership and authority at home? Not if he's married to a woman who's had her "consciousness raised." Should he open doors for his wife or give a lady his seat on the train or rise when she enters the room? Who knows? Will he march off to defend his homeland in times of war, or will his wife be the one to fight on foreign soil? Should he wear jewelry and satin shoes or carry a purse? Alas, is there *anything* that marks him as different from his female counterpart?[31]

Nothing revealed the threat of feminism more to its critics than a newspaper photograph, taken at the beginning of Desert Storm, showing a young mother kissing her infant goodbye as she headed off to war. As Heritage Foundation trustee Midge Decter noted, the photograph spoke volumes about the mess society had become and was as obscene as any pornography ever could be. Decter explained that the photograph was not about the equality of women, but about the madness that had overcome so many U.S. families. As a result of feminism, many families have become what she termed "a place of profound disorder."[32]

Many in the Promise Keepers' movement view feminism in similarly derogatory terms. Tony Evans, who speaks at many Promise Keepers' rallies, complains that the leadership roles of men have been taken away by feminists. In a chapter entitled "No More Sissified Males," he explains that "feminists of the more aggressive persuasion are frustrated women unable to find the proper male leadership."[33] If women would accept their God-given roles, order would be restored to the family.

THE LIBERAL WELFARE AGENDA

According to the religious right, welfare has accelerated the disintegration of the family in the United States. It has been faulted for contributing to crime, illegitimacy, and fatherless children and for eroding the Protestant work ethic and traditional family values. Notes former Christian Coalition executive director Ralph Reed, welfare has perpetuated the "cycle of family decay by subsidizing the movement of husbands and fathers out of the home."[34] In this way, government is seen as having supported policies that do not encourage marriage, making it harder for the traditional family to function. Ultimately, the result is the collapse of the family.[35] According to Pat Robertson, the billions of dollars designated for welfare have only worsened poverty and promoted illegitimacy, unstable families, and a debilitating dependency. He believes that subsidizing the poor only encourages them not to support themselves. The goal of conservatives, claims Robertson, is not only to do away with liberalism, but to get rid of "the entire socialist, welfare state."[36]

Conservative critics of welfare charge that, in the last thirty years, the welfare system has "paid for non-work and non-marriage," with the result that the rate of both unemployment and unwed mothers has risen. Indeed, the work ethic has been deliberately undermined, and illegitimacy has been underwritten. The more money we throw at welfare, the more those in need of welfare increase, or so the reasoning goes.[37] Welfare programs in the United States came about as aid for what was termed "the worthy poor." Even in the early part of the twentieth century, the debate was configured along the lines of controlling the behavior of those who received help. Welfare was seen as an effort to "better" immigrants. At the base of this justification always lurked the suspicion that those who needed welfare were somehow at fault for their poverty, and if only they had been better managers, better citizens, or better workers, they would not need the help of the state.

Dissatisfaction with welfare can be traced to the early 1960s, when Barry Goldwater and members of the John Birch Society associated the War on Poverty with communism, especially targeting the Aid to Families with Dependent Children (AFDC) program as an example of how the excesses of liberalism destroy the social order and eventually lead to socialism (which in turn leads to communism).[38] They believed that most, if not all, of the ills affecting society would be nonexistent if it were not for welfare.

By the 1990s, those who opposed welfare included a growing number on the religious right whose pro-family movement helped to frame the debate. Phyllis Schlafly's Eagle Forum, in particular, pointed out the conflict over the role of women—home versus work—that is part of the debate. Schlafly argued that welfare encouraged fathers to abandon their responsibilities in that it took over the male role in the family. Furthermore, she charged that welfare only encouraged the formation of nontraditional families, resulting in increasing numbers of poverty-stricken children; this then only perpetuated the cycle of poverty. To her, the welfare programs of the 1960s were "morally wrong."[39] Gary Bauer added his voice to Schlafly's, noting that there was a correlation between the availability of welfare assistance and the tendency of women to bring fatherless children into the world.[40] The Heritage Foundation also cited "America's number one social problem" as being the "catastrophic rise of illegitimacy."[41] The analysis of the religious right focused almost exclusively on issues of immorality; to them, welfare begot illegitimacy, and illegitimacy begot poverty. And this immorality was located almost exclusively in African American and Hispanic communities. In this way race and gender played formative roles in constructing the stereotype of an unworthy recipient of welfare. Ultimately, claimed the religious right, welfare—which encouraged irresponsibility and rewarded a lack of personal initiative—was responsible for the breakup of the family.[42]

Welfare, far from helping the family, was causing single parents and children who were part of the welfare system to suffer as well. Robert Rector of the Heritage Foundation argued that the welfare system is akin to free passage on a bus going nowhere:

[Welfare] is riddled with perverse incentives that discourage work and marriage while encouraging illegitimate birth and long-term dependency. Precisely because single-parent family life is much harder on children, as well as on their mothers and the broader society, it is no kindness for government to make either single parenthood or long-term dependency easier and more common. Given the perverse incentives of the traditional welfare system, millions of parents and their children cannot escape to a better life. Liberal welfare undermines their upward economic mobility and eventual independence, but also robs them of hope for the future and reinforces spiritual despair.[43]

A 1995 report entitled "Public Attitudes toward Welfare and Welfare Reform" notes that welfare policy has become primarily a focus of moral concern. Those polled (primarily white) responded to the topic with an unusual sense of "moral outrage" and were overwhelmingly concerned with the moral message conveyed by the welfare system. They viewed the welfare system as "an affront to their own commitment to hard work and willingness to play by the rules."[44] The subject of welfare evoked sentiments of righteous anger from those polled—an attitude that is widespread. The existence of welfare is seen as a threat to the traditional family structure. Single motherhood, which seems to go hand in hand with conservative descriptions of welfare, is viewed as pathological at best and as a moral failing at worst.

THE GODLESS IDEOLOGY OF RELATIVISM

In the late 1990s, the religious right sounded the alarm that, once again, the cold war is alive and well. The enemy, in this instance, is no longer communism, but relativism. Gary Bauer of the Family Research Council is one of the strongest voices against this ideology. He describes it as a chameleon in many colors: "At the individual level, it says, 'If it feels good, do it.' At the social level, it says, 'What's right for you isn't right for me.' At the international level, it says, 'They do things differently in foreign countries. Who are we to judge?'"[45]

Relativism, like its forebears, is pegged as being a sure path to "social breakdown and self-destruction." Evidence of this, note many on the religious right, is apparent in the lack of educational achievement in the nation's schools, violence within schools, pornography, rising numbers of broken homes, and the religious persecution of Christians in the United States. Because relativism has gained such a stronghold in public discourse, relativism is blamed for strangling the discussion of moral values. Bauer pleads for pro-family Christians to take action against this new threat to the country.[46]

Tolerance

Closely related to the threat of relativism is the concept of tolerance. A relatively new threat on the horizon of the religious right, tolerance is targeted as another liberal "feel good," politically correct tool of ideology. The problem is that to folks on the religious right, "tolerance" precludes any sort of judgment against immoral behavior. They claim that "previously despised forms of deviancy, degradation, and aberrant behavior" are accepted and that the discourse over serious moral issues suffers if tolerance is permitted to undermine the traditional values that are part of our nation's history.[47] James Dobson quotes an unidentified writer on the subject: "Tolerance is the virtue of people who do not believe in anything." He goes on to warn that those who advocate tolerance risk becoming so accepting of everything that evil goes unrecognized and unopposed. In such circumstances, the moral collapse of the nation cannot be far off.[48] Another writer, questioning the meaning of tolerance, admitted that if "intolerance" meant the ostracizing of those with "different" values, obviously, it would be wrong. After all, Jesus always included those on the margins of society. And yet, argued the writer, he would never have accepted any sort of "destructive lifestyles or actions that harmed others." What would happen, the religious right often queries, in a society that tolerated everything?[49]

Not surprisingly, the concept of tolerance is most often debated around the issues related to sexuality. The concept of tolerance, in part, pertains to the sexual revolution of the 1960s. The religious right believes that the sexual revolution sowed false promises and contributed to the decline of the family. Unplanned pregnancies, sexually transmitted diseases, abortions, broken homes, pornography, and "an orchestrated effort to force everyone—especially young people—to affirm homosexuality as normal and desirable" have flowed from the age of "free love."[50] The term "compassion" is often used interchangeably with "tolerance." In a Family Research Council report, readers are warned that the emphasis on compassion, espoused by groups advocating civil rights for lesbian and gay people, can be distracting, if not downright misleading: "Concentrate on the suffering of the victims and you will forget to oppose the kind of conduct that leads to such a monstrous malady."[51]

While charging that contemporary culture prefers tolerance over moral absolutes, the religious right also makes a comparison to ancient Israel whose "presumptuous tolerance . . . led to violence and destruction." The tolerance of sin blinds one to its danger. And as ancient Israel reaped the consequences of its tolerance, so too will contemporary society. Ultimately, according to the religious right, there is "no freedom for those who follow the flesh and ignore God's truth."[52] Tolerance over moral absolutes inevitably results in destruction.

The threats to the institution of the traditional family, as we have seen, are varied. The homosexual agenda, the feminist agenda, the liberal welfare agenda, godless relativism, tolerance, and others too numerous to mention in these pages combine to create what the religious right sees as an overall societal trend toward decay and damnation. What, then, can turn the tide?

SOLUTIONS

What is clear in the debate over how to handle the moral decline in the culture and the concomitant threats to the family is that the solutions to today's problems, according to the religious right, will be found only if America confesses its sins and returns to faith in God. The chaos that characterizes society cannot be solved only economically. Ralph Reed maintains that we are faced with "a collection of moral problems that require moral solutions"; the profamily agenda is exactly where these moral solutions can be found.[53]

Interestingly enough, Reed draws on the Social Gospel to justify the political involvement of evangelical Christians. Quoting Reinhold Niebuhr—"the purpose of politics is to establish justice in a fallen world"—Reed declares that to alleviate social ills, faithful people must participate in the political arena. While advocating the use of the political system, Reed cautions that such use be combined with efforts to limit the scope of government influence. Political action at the local and state levels helps guard against the excessive power of a centralized federal government.[54]

Defining the Family

The family, "consisting in and springing from the union for life of one man and one woman in the holy estate of matrimony," is understood by the religious right to be the "foundational institution of human society."[55] While advocating the "traditional" family form as the only form that is acceptable and, ultimately, the only form that will pull the country out of the moral abyss it has fallen into, members of the religious right are curiously not in agreement among themselves about the exact meaning of the traditional family. This lack of agreement is evident in their ideological conceptions of family; the literature on the subject focuses on several different definitions of family, ranging from Puritan to Victorian (as we saw in chapter 1) to what political scientist Michael Lienesch has characterized as postwar images describing family as "'church,' 'haven,' and 'corporation.'"[56] Regardless, the form of the contemporary family is not in doubt: it is made up of a monogamous, heterosexual married man and woman, plus children. Furthermore, in the traditional family the lines of power are clear: men are the leaders, decision makers, and ultimate authorities; women are helpmates who stand by their men and submit to the inherent wisdom of male leadership; children are obedient. Gender roles never deviate from the proscribed norm, and feminism and homosexuality are seen as forces that are intentionally damaging to the well-being of the family.

In response to the movement to legalize marriage among lesbian and gay couples, the religious right has argued that U.S. family law has traditionally looked at the term "family" as applying only to those who are related by blood, marriage, or adoption, and attempts were made to limit the meaning of the term accordingly. The concern, of course, was to make certain that those who did not fit that definition, such as unmarried heterosexual couples, single mothers and their children, and lesbian and gay couples, could not be recognized as being family.

The White House Conference on the Family, held during the Carter presidency, drew fire from many conservative Christians who feared that the true agenda was to change the meaning of the terms "marriage" and "family" to include lesbian and gay people. The delegates to the conference who identified themselves as "pro-family" argued that to say that the term "family" included gay and lesbian people was tantamount to including the Manson Family in that definition. As determined as the liberals were to include other types of families alongside the traditional type, the pro-family faction was equally determined "to hold onto the real true meaning of the genuine family, as God intended it to be."[57] Ultimately, the attendees failed to agree on a definition of "family." In 1980, James Dobson related that God had told him traditional family life should be on the top of everyone's agenda. Dobson paraphrased God's words to him: "If America is going to survive the incredible stresses and dangers it now faces, it will be because husbands and fathers again place their families at the highest level on their system of priorities, reserving a portion of their time and energy for leadership within their homes!"[58]

In Defense of Marriage

Organizations that fall under the umbrella of the religious right view marriage as the "bedrock of how we are defined as a people and as a culture."[59] They often point to history and maintain that no society has ever functioned without the institution of marriage. In fact, historically, whenever marriage was "cheapened," the social order began to unravel.[60] Pat Fagan of the Heritage Foundation theorizes that separating the sex act from its primary biological purpose resulted in the destruction of society. The discussion has evolved from birth control in the 1960s to abortion in the 1970s to gender roles in the 1980s to homosexuality in the 1990s. Fagan squarely lays the blame for the current state of affairs at the feet of birth control. The only way to "pull the nation back" to where it should be is for Christians to consider abstinence within marriage.[61]

In the Heritage Foundation's *Candidate's Briefing Book*, Fagan maintains that when the percentage of single-parent families in any given community reaches around 30 percent, the result is the breakdown of the community and a corresponding rise in the crime rate.[62] One solution is the increased focus on state legislation specifically designed to shore up traditional marital commitments. "Covenant Marriage," a voluntary agreement under which men and women legally commit themselves to a more permanent marriage, allows divorce only under certain conditions. In such marriages, no-fault divorce laws would no longer apply. Ralph Reed has noted that such marriage reform would encourage couples to stay married, especially if children were involved. And if legal waiting periods before a divorce could be granted were in place, the law would, once again, be more supportive of marriage than of divorce.[63] The Southern Baptist Convention exulted, "Such public policies . . . aim to strengthen the marriage commitment and to reverse the trend of the disintegration of the nuclear family."[64] Marriage is understood to be absolutely essential to stability and continuity because the kinship that comes from marriage provides family names, genealogical history, and property as well as acting as a way of securing the commitment of men to the responsibilities of fatherhood and providing a channel for obligations to the wider community.[65]

In keeping with this view, the Southern Baptists reworded their statement of Baptist Faith at their June 1998 annual convention to read as follows: "Marriage is the uniting of one man and one woman in covenant commitment for a lifetime. It is God's unique gift to reveal the union between Christ and His church, and to provide for the man and the woman in marriage the framework for intimate companionship, the channel for sexual expression according to biblical standards, and the means for procreation of the human race."[66]

Similarly, in a recent publication, the Ecumenical Coalition on Women and Society (ECWS) affirmed that God created two complementary genders and, furthermore, that particular configuration of human sexuality is the foundation of society. They also celebrated the "healthy relationships" that embody that configuration, namely, "the divinely ordained covenant of marriage between one man and one woman prepared to bear and rear each succeeding generation of children."[67]

The Family Research Council, organized around the subject of defending the traditional family, asserts that the communities are healthiest that have the most intact, traditional, marriage-based families. At the center of family life is marriage, which is understood to be the building block of civilization. The unique nature of marriage requires legal and cultural protection because it is "indispensable to civilized life." Robert Knight, director of cultural studies at the Family Research Council, notes that marriage provides society with much more than any other relationship; it is a stabilizing force for sexuality and provides the best possible environment in which to rear children: "No other relationship transforms young men and women into more productive, less selfish, and more mature husbands and wives, and fathers and mothers, than marriage. No other relationship affords children the best economic, emotional and psychological environment."[68] Our wandering from the acceptance of marriage as the one, true way of being in relation—argue its defenders—has allowed the social problems including illegitimacy, divorce, sexually transmitted diseases, and crime to spiral out of control. In short, marriage is the cement that holds families together; without it, communities and the culture as a whole disintegrate. Therefore, according to Knight, traditional marriage—between a man and a woman—is "a non-negotiable necessity."[69]

The move to recognize lesbian or gay marriages is greeted with arguments organized around nature: sexuality is firmly imprinted in our natures and is rooted in the biological fact that only a man and a woman can make a baby. This, so the argument goes, is the notion of marriage that deserves special protection, respect, and defense; this notion of marriage is the building block of the nation. In a Capitol Hill briefing on the Defense of Marriage Act, Hadley Arkes of the Family Research Council argued for that notion:

The irony then is that the notion of marriage cannot accommodate couples of the same sex without so altering the cast or character of marriage that it will cease to be that special relation, which seems to be the object of such deep craving now for so many people. Once the notion of marriage is broadened in that way, it will simply not be tenable any longer to hold up marriage, in the laws, as a relation that deserves a special place, a special commendation—a special effort to sustain and promote it. And indeed, we fear that the movement to gay marriage is fueled in part by a desire to remove that special standing in principle—to deny that there is anything about marriage that deserves a special respect, or any favored standing in the law. . . . The question of marriage for gays or lesbians, or rights of adoption for gay couples, take on their importance strategically: They provide further occasions for moving the law to pronounce that homosexuality is, in the current phrase, "virtually normal," that homosexuality cannot stand on any lesser plane of legitimacy than that sexuality "imprinted in our natures."[70]

The bottom line of the issue is that if two women can marry each other or two men can marry each other, then any special recognition or protection of traditional marriage with all of its rights and privileges ceases. Ralph Reed maintains that any attempt to tinker with "the meaning of marriage when the traditional two-parent, marriage-based family is already an endangered species" is not the better part of wisdom. Such tinkering, rather than helping society, further damages its central institution. Society would be better served, argues Reed, if traditional marriage were recognized as deserving special protection by the government, thereby excluding the possibility that other sorts of relationships would sneak in and be defined under its rubric.[71] Safeguarding the narrow definition of marriage defends the institution of the family and protects the ordered structure of power and privilege granted exclusively to heterosexual unions.

SEX AND MALE AUTHORITY

The social theory of the religious right has male authority as its basis. Armed with the Genesis account of the creation of Adam and Eve, members of the religious right argue that since God made man in his image, God intended men to be the authorities from the beginning. According to this interpretation, Adam was commanded to rule the world. It is with this understanding in mind that James Dobson makes clear that the survival of America depends on the presence of male leadership in homes across the country; indeed, "husbands hold the keys to the preservation of the family."[72] God has given men this responsibility for leadership. Despite the contemporary questioning of and confusion surrounding male roles (brought on by the feminist movement), man's duty is still to dominate or, more gently put, take over the leadership role. Feminism, claims Dobson, has attacked "maleness" and damaged the image of what qualities make a good husband and father.[73] Feminist women, by their insistence on equality between the sexes, gave men permission to abdicate their responsibilities. Pat Robertson believes strongly that the husband is always the head of the household; the many problems experienced by contemporary families would disappear if only women would come to their senses and be submissive to their husbands.[74] Even though Promise Keepers, as an organization, claims not to have an official position on male headship, Bill McCartney maintains that "Almighty God has mandated that the man take the spiritual lead in the home."[75]

The pro-family movement further leans on biological and psychological theories to contend that the male nature is to exercise authority. Tim LaHaye, a fundamentalist Christian and author of marriage manuals, argues that since men differ from women physically—primarily because of the hormone testosterone—they are endowed with the characteristics of "aggressiveness, dominance, ambition, and sexual initiative." Furthermore, differences in brain formation predispose the males of the species to be better able to exercise leadership than the females. If a male infant does not receive enough testosterone in utero, contends LaHaye, he will be prone to exhibit "feminine characteristics" and will become "passive."[76]

Phyllis Schlafly affirms these arguments in her book *The Power of the Christian Woman*. She insists that men are psychologically geared to be "rational" as opposed to "emotional." Men, therefore, are biologically predisposed through a "boldness of the imagination" to engage in "higher intellectual activities"; women, according to Schlafly, "tend more toward conformity than men—which is why they often excel in such disciplines as spelling and punctuation." Women, she declares, should never presume to act like men. Any attempt to do so is tantamount to forcing a left-handed child to become right-handed.[77]

Many writers of this genre understand men as being shaped by their sexuality. LaHaye believes that men are destined to be sexual aggressors because of the "constant production of sperm and seminal fluid." That is why, according to LaHaye, the male sex drive is almost uncontrollable; it is "almost volcanic" and will "erupt at the slightest provocation."[78] In other words, men are held captive to their biological drives. Though the work in which these words were written was published in the late 1960s, this attitude remains present in the approach of the literature of the religious right to issues pertaining to male/female relationships. Controlling—or taming—male sexuality, then, becomes the goal of marriage. When subjected to the limits of marriage and family, male sexuality is transformed from a "volcanic" sexuality to a sexuality that is a social good: it is transformed to a sexuality that is protective of those who are weaker and thereby creates a stable atmosphere. Man as the leader of and provider for his family becomes an asset to society—even an enthusiastic cog in the wheel of the Protestant work ethic.

Today's social climate contributes to the confusion of men regarding their roles. As Lienesch notes, though described theoretically as sexually aggressive, the males of the species "are in practice fairly flaccid fellows," insecure about what their roles should be as men.[79] This insecurity is most often blamed on women who usurp their husbands' prerogative to rule. The economic need for women to work outside the home after marriage increases men's insecurity; men are no longer able to be the sole support of their families. LaHaye claims that working outside the home encourages a sense of "independence and self-sufficiency which God did not intend a married woman to have." This contributes, he believes, to the rising divorce rate.[80]

Aggressive women, particularly aggressive Christian wives, appear to undermine their husbands' male egos. Christian women who take on outside responsibilities and prominent roles in the workplace deprive their husbands of the chance to provide them with support and protection, thus creating men who are insecure in their male roles. Such men are, it seems, becoming increasingly "feminized" and are at risk of losing their manhood. Promise Keepers' speaker Tony Evans believes that a national crisis has been brought on by "the feminization of the American male." He purports that a misinterpretation of the concept of manhood has produced an entire nation of "sissified" men who gave away their role as leaders of their families, thus forcing their wives to take over.[81] The effect of wives having to take their husbands' places has added fuel to the feminist movement that, the religious right charges, champions the ideal of the strong, independent, and assertive woman at the expense of the strong, independent, and assertive man. The problem with this ideal in the eyes of the right is that strong, independent, and assertive women make their husbands subconsciously feel as if they are "married to a second mother."[82] Expounds James Dobson, when male energies are not directed toward the support of a home, such scourges as substance abuse, sexual immorality, aggressive behavior, and job stresses are likely to run rampant throughout the society. That, according to Dobson, spells the beginning of the end.[83]

Charles Stanley, writing in the late 1970s, maintained that the only way to keep men from being feminized and infantilized is that women must submit to male rule. He added, in tones reminiscent of today's Promise Keepers, that the best way to motivate a wife to be submissive is to "serve her."[84] According to Anita Bryant's former husband, Bob Green, the Christian husband is obligated to assume the leadership role in his family because God has directed him to do so.[85] God has given the husband the responsibility "to provide for, to protect and to lead his family." And a wife must, therefore, submit graciously to her husband's leadership.[86]

More recently, the Promise Keepers have highlighted the need for men to take back the reins of spiritual leadership in their families. The husband/father should be the head of the household and the family leader, but should lead gently, surrendering his own ego to serve his spouse. In one of the most quoted passages of

Promise Keepers' literature, Tony Evans, a regular Promise Keepers' speaker and chaplain to the Dallas Mavericks basketball team, urged husbands to take charge: "The first thing you do is sit down with your wife and say something like this: 'Honey, I've made a terrible mistake. I've given you my role. I gave up leading this family, and I forced you to take my place. Now I must reclaim that role.' Don't misunderstand what I'm saying here. I'm not suggesting that you *ask* for your role back, I'm urging you to *take it back*."[87]

Evans also instructed women to give the leadership role back to their husbands and let their husbands be men, if they were so willing. After all, as James Dobson told a stadium full of "hairy-chested testosterone-driven" Promise Keepers in 1993, nothing is more important "to a godly woman" than that her husband be a spiritual leader for the family.[88] Ed Cole, president of the Christian Men's Network, underlined the importance that men in general, and Promise Keepers in particular, acting like men should do the following:

Act more like a man! Why? Because when a man acts like a child it forces his wife to act like his mother. And when a man forces his wife to act like his mother, she does two things for him. She makes decisions for him and she corrects him. Now there's a problem with that! . . . If your wife no longer trusts your word, she can no longer respect you and she can no longer submit to you. And if she can no longer respect you and submit to you, then she no longer wants to bear your name.[89]

In order for a man to claim effectively his God-given, male authority, a woman must be submissive. Male authority and female independence were never meant to coexist. Male authority and female powerlessness were!

FEMALE POWERLESSNESS

As feminists have confused the issue of male sex-role identity, so too are they accused of having sowed seeds of confusion regarding female sex-role identity. The result, according to critics of the feminist movement, is that the traditional concept of femininity has been ridiculed. This has resulted in the occupation of home-maker and mother being seen as less valuable than the career of a woman who works outside the home. According to some, it has produced a rise in the rate of depression among women. Explains Dobson:

> God created us as sexual beings, and any confusion in that under-standing is devastating to the self-concept. Those most affected are the women who are inextricably identified with the traditional role, those who are "stranded" in a homemaking responsibility. Thus, wives and mothers have found themselves wondering, "Who am I?" and then nervously asking, "Who *should* I be?"[90]

Thus, feminists are blamed for inciting unrest in the hearts of women across the nation. When women question gender roles and develop the desire to choose what they do with their lives (whether it be homemaking and mothering or working outside the home), the tradition of women submitting to their husbands comes under question as well. The advocates of traditional roles insist that a clear distinction between the roles of the sexes is criti-cal to defeating the forces of revolution that seek to dismantle the traditional family and question which relationships should be considered marriages. Without distinctive roles, we blaspheme the One who created us. Male headship and female submission are therefore critically important to the survival of the Christian way.

The submission of women is justified by writers of the Chris-tian right by Eve's fall from grace. Since then, women have been destined for the pain of bearing children and assigned the role of assisting their male partners in the task of reproduction. The bio-logical argument—that women's physiology preordains that they will embrace maternity—is central to maintaining the subservi-ent status of the so-called weaker sex. The ultimate female sin, in these authors' eyes, is for women to avoid motherhood via birth control or worse—abortion. Beverly LaHaye asserts that women are naturally domestic, since the home is but "an extension of the mother's womb," and motherhood in itself represents "the high-est form of femininity."[91] More recently, Midge Decter proclaimed that one cannot fool Mother Nature. Marriage and family are not choices, but represent the bedrock of human existence, a fact, she claims, that more and more young women are coming to realize.[92] Nothing—not even national emergencies—should interrupt the bond of mother-child relationships; the recent resolve of the Southern Baptist Convention, joined by Focus on the Family, to oppose women being assigned to combat positions in wartime reflects this sentiment.[93]

Along with men being seen as the sexual aggressors, women are viewed as the sexual responders, or the passive of the two genders. This approach assumes the complementarity theory of sexuality. This theory posits that "without women men were incomplete and without men women were incomplete. From the opposite gender came what the other lacked; the two genders thus provided a balance to one another."[94] The complementarity theory of sexuality runs throughout the literature of the Christian right; it justifies the stronger sex drive of men while at the same time raising up the role of women as bearing responsibility for domesticating the male of the species. This responsibility, apparently, can be fulfilled only by submitting to male headship. Furthermore, any departure from the complementarity formula of male plus female places the entire structure of society at risk.

Interestingly enough, while asserting that women must submit to the leadership of men, the Christian right also faults women for being too sexually passive in their marriages, especially when the Christian marriage is headed toward failure. Phyllis Schlafly advises, "The Christian Woman builds her power by using her womanhood, not by denying or suppressing it."[95]

If the married woman is faulted for her own marriage problems, the single woman is seen to be even more of a threat on several counts. First, she is perceived to be in competition with married women (thus posing a threat to the institution of marriage); second, she is in competition in the workplace for men's jobs, thereby shaking the security of the fragile male ego. (This argument was used extensively by Phyllis Schlafly against the Equal Rights Amendment.) Single women also run the risk of being labeled lesbian, and the single woman is carefully warned to avoid this perception at all costs.[96]

Ultimately, women are charged with saving the social order. This can be done only if women will surrender themselves to the spiritual leadership of their husbands, making their husbands' contentment their vocation. This submission is understood as coming naturally to women (thus, feminism is seen as being unnatural). Tim LaHaye elaborates that "God would not have commanded a woman to submit unless He had instilled in her a psychic mechanism which would find it comfortable to do so." For the woman who might balk at such reasoning, he adds that "subjection," after all, is "a command of God and her refusal to comply with this command is an act of disobedience."[97]

In creating an atmosphere of gracious submission, James Dobson urges that wives take heed of their husbands' need for tranquillity at home and work diligently to create a refreshing oasis. This familiar theme of home as haven from the heartless, cruel world is a familiar one as we have seen, and it harkens back to the Victorian era. Today, the trumpet call for home as a peaceful, safe haven continues to be heard. Professional pressures are so severe, explains Dobson, that the home must be "a haven to which a man can return." A wise woman will make her home what her spouse needs for it to be.[98]

Ending Welfare As We Know It

Representative Henry Hyde insists that government welfare policies deliberately move resources from what works (the two-parent family) to what does not work (the poor, single mother who must rely on others to have even a chance of surviving): "Let me state the obvious: The only reason there is a pro-family movement in this country is that there has long been an anti-family movement. It's never called that, but there it is."[99] Not only does welfare encourage single parenthood, but it is labeled as what impedes the formation of families and continues to wreak havoc on society.[100]

In the debate over welfare reform, the issues that concern the religious right—namely, those that revolve around the traditional family—are paramount. The discourse reflects the pervasive struggle over changing family structures, the role of women in the family and in society as a whole, race relations, and the role of government in our daily lives. Tied in with these issues is the nostalgic longing for the imagined security of years gone by when real men provided for their families and sought to attain the upward mobility promised by the American Dream. According to Ralph Reed, there are three fundamental requirements for upward mobility in America: "graduate from high school, get a job and keep it, and get married."[101] According to Reed, intact families function as the best Department of Health, Education, and Welfare.[102] Since single-parent households inevitably beget violence and juvenile delinquency, the solution must be to strengthen the two-parent, traditional family. This can be done only by refusing to subsidize financially single-parent families. Thus, welfare reform, noted Reed, must promote "work, savings, marriage, and personal responsibility."[103]

The welfare reform act of 1996 incorporated conservative proposals. Among the most important were placing time limits on welfare benefits and requiring welfare recipients to find work outside the home. As of January 1, 1997, welfare recipients were limited to a total of five years of federal cash assistance and are required to work within two years of signing onto the welfare rolls. Cash welfare has now been converted into block grants for states, which are penalized if they fail to develop their own plans for moving welfare recipients into the workforce. States may also choose to deny further aid to those who give birth to children while receiving welfare benefits. The religious right now seeks to abolish welfare benefits completely for unwed teenage mothers. In this way, taxpayers would no longer be underwriting irresponsible behavior and the resulting illegitimate children. Some have even suggested that the children whose parents are unable to support them could be removed from their homes.

The conservative mind-set in relation to welfare is that the greater social good must be promoted by a combination of the efforts of private charities, the safeguarding of the traditional family, and the protection of an unregulated market economy. Indeed, in the context of welfare reform, restoring the primacy of the institution of marriage ranks as the primary social goal for makers of policy. For the first time, the new legislation addresses the problem of illegitimacy and makes ending it a national objective.[104]

Ethicist Pamela Brubaker maintains that from this viewpoint, poverty is understood as resulting from personal irresponsibility and, therefore, cannot be blamed on any failure of the capitalist economy.[105] In this context, those who exhibit personal initiative are the ones who will survive and even thrive. The others who remain chronically unable to pull themselves up by their own boot-straps—because they were not wearing any boots to begin with—will be lost.

The agenda of the religious right now centers on restoring the missing male to the picture, assuming that this will strengthen families and, by that strengthening, will end poverty. If men can be held accountable for indiscriminately fathering children, then the problem of poverty will cease to exist. If that does not work, single mothers on welfare, who remain unconnected to any male breadwinner, could go out and get jobs (known popularly as "workfare"); then they will become self-sufficient and will no longer need the support of welfare.

Another key aspect of conservative welfare policy assumes that churches and other private charities will be able to take the place of the welfare state. This was evident during the 1980s with George Bush's oft-repeated references to the "thousand points of light." These points of light, Bush maintained, were the points at which the American people took seriously the commandment to love their neighbors and reached out in a spirit of charity. Since then, whenever conservative politicians are asked who will provide a safety net for those who otherwise would fall between the cracks, they have responded that private charitable organizations, more particularly faith-based organizations, will take up the slack. It is also assumed that such organizations would do a better job and would be more compassionate.[106] By transferring responsibility for poor people from the government to the churches and other nonprofit organizations, the religious right hopes that Christian morality will be able to bring the epidemic of illegitimacy under control.

AMERICA, A CHRISTIAN NATION

The assertion that "America is a Christian nation" is one widely reputed to be held among the religious right. As a faith statement about the covenant relationship that God has with the nation, it can be seen as an interpretation of the collective national experience. We hear this invoked especially surrounding issues of prayer in schools and other public places and over debates on homosexuality and abortion. Many people believe this to be a historical and political fact. House Majority Whip Tom DeLay declared at the Christian Coalition's 1998 Road to Victory Conference that "the Constitution of the United States was written by the Founding Fathers as a model of the Bible, and comes directly out of the Bible."[107]

One aspect of the understanding that America is a Christian nation is that some, such as Beverly LaHaye, champion the notion that the government should be run by those who espouse Christian values: "Religion and politics do mix. America is a nation based on biblical principles. Christian values dominate our government. The test of those values is the Bible. Politicians who do not use the Bible to guide their public and private lives do not belong in office."[108]

At the 1998 meeting of the Council for National Policy,[109] Howard Phillips (long known as a Christian reconstructionist and champion of the U.S. Taxpayers Party)[110] urged those gathered not to "surrender the Christian legal heritage which undergirds our civic order." In reference to the issues of abortion and homosexuality, he added that not even the Supreme Court has the power to legalize "what God has declared to be illegal." Federal subsidies to "practitioners of buggery" for AIDS education should be cut in order to nip the militant homosexual agenda in the bud, and all abortions, not just partial birth abortions, should be outlawed by applying the constitutional provision that "no person may be deprived of life except by due process of law" to those as yet unborn.[111] His views are firmly entrenched in the understanding that the United States government at the time of its founding had an explicitly Christian legal system, which was traceable to biblical roots. Society is currently troubled, he believes, because the original biblical roots of government have been ignored.

Pat Robertson had somewhat backed away from the Christian nation vision, if only because of the fact that he views U.S. society as a moral failure. His grave dissatisfaction with this state of affairs was clear in such comments as, "We had in America a Christian nation. It has been taken away from us."[112] He believes that without guiding religious principles, people tend "to be immoral and careless about marital obligations." Human nature is such, he maintains, that if opportunity arises, people will lie, steal, engage in substance abuse, and commit acts of violence. The threat of punishment is not a deterrent; only religious principles can provide that.[113] More recently, at the 1998 Road to Victory Conference, Robertson spoke about making America a nation of God. "The Christian Coalition is going to fight the battle for morality in America and we're going to see this nation come back to God," he said. Ralph Reed echoed the sentiment, proclaiming that his calling was "to restore America to be one nation under God."[114] Chuck Colson, formerly convicted of a Watergate-related felony and now head of a prison ministry, declared that "Christians have always been the best citizens."[115]

When speaking to the gathering of thirty-nine thousand male pastors in 1996, Bill McCartney proclaimed that "whoever stands with the Messiah will rule with him," and he urged the clergy to take the nation for Jesus.[116] Similarly, James Dobson has referred consistently to America as a Christian nation. He firmly maintains that the church has a duty to hold a government leader accountable and that any who act against God's will should be called back publicly to biblical fidelity. For this cause, Dobson has made known that he is prepared to give his life.[117]

RETURN TO THE PAST

A constant theme of the religious right is returning society to the days when America was great. Then, and only then, will America be great again—or so the reasoning goes. Robertson's 1988 presidential campaign was focused around this theme. His campaign slogan—"Restore the Greatness of America through Moral Strength"—called forth the image of an America restored to the way he imagined it to have been. In speaking about the involvement of Christian people in the political arena, Robertson exclaimed (in 1990) that people of faith would be in politics until America was "brought back to its founding principles." During a

1995 speech at the Law School of William and Mary, he opined, "We want our history back. We want our tradition back. We want our country back." He added that the people of faith would "work for a time when this nation is once again one nation under God."[118]

The theme of returning to a time when America was truly great is closely connected to the theme of America as a Christian nation. The grace and the good fortune that the country has enjoyed are directly attributable to the fact that it has been in good favor with God. According to Robertson, the number one status of America in the world came about because those who founded this country "made a solemn covenant that they would be the people of God and that this would be a Christian nation."[119] Ralph Reed, usually more nuanced in his statements, declared in 1993 during an address to the Ethics and Public Policy Center, "What most religious conservatives really want is to reclaim some strengths of the America that most of us grew up in, the post–World War II America that was proud, militarily strong, morally sound and looked up to by the rest of the world."[120] The turmoil of the 1960s and 1970s and the subsequent movements of African Americans, women, and lesbian women and gay men for liberation are generally blamed for the disintegration of that utopian America.

According to the religious right, America's salvation can come about only through a return to the traditions that made America great. Only the restoration of family values to the mainstream American consciousness will stem the tide of the moral decay that has swept over the land. A massive effort has been mounted to achieve that goal, and the troops have been called forth to do battle.

CHRISTIAN SOLDIERS GO FORTH TO WAR

Pat Robertson wrote,

> The strategy against the American radical left should be the same as General Douglas MacArthur employed against the Japanese in the Pacific. . . . Bypass their strongholds, then surround them, isolate them, bombard them, then blast the individuals out of their power bunkers with hand-to-hand combat. The battle for Iwo Jima was not pleasant, but our troops won it. The battle to regain the soul of America won't be pleasant either, but we will win it![121]

War imagery is present in the literature of the religious right. Some savvy leaders have attempted to explain away the language, as applying only to warfare in the spiritual realm, claiming that war imagery is biblically based. Ralph Reed, who at the time was executive director of the Christian Coalition, realized in the early 1990s that his use of military metaphors was too easily misinterpreted by the liberal media as being incendiary and thus was a liability to the organization. He decided that military rhetoric was not appropriate for a Christian organization because "it lacked the redemptive grace that should always characterize our words and deeds," and he immediately sent word to the grassroots chapters of the Christian Coalition to replace war imagery with sports- and weather-related imagery.[122]

Evidently, he forgot to tell his boss. In 1991, Pat Robertson predicted that in "raising an army who cares," by the turn of the century, the Christian Coalition would be "the most powerful political organization in America."[123] A year later, Robertson reiterated the necessity for Christian people to take back control of society's institutions, and he warned that there would be plenty of confrontations and that they would be unpleasant and "at times physically bloody."[124]

Since Reed has left the Christian Coalition, resolve around limiting militaristic language has weakened, if not entirely disappeared. At the 1998 Road to Victory Conference, militarism was alive and well. Rabbi Daniel Lapin, one of the plenary speakers, declared that a religious war is going on in the United States between the Judeo-Christian faith and secular liberalism and that God has made clear that people of faith are to "go out and fight."[125] Don Hodel, when praising Pat Robertson's contributions to the movement, noted that Robertson had "raised a hidden army to take over the GOP." Indeed, the army was to take over more than the GOP; it was to take over the entire country. Hodel added, "We are determined to take over the culture."[126] Charlton Heston, the keynote banquet speaker, referred to "the bloody stain of cultural warfare." He further pontificated: "Sabers are rattling in America's mild mannered living rooms. They want it back. They want the America they built. They want to be white without feeling guilty and to prosper without feeling blamed."[127] Even more chilling was the evening's entertainment, provided by the Liberty University Choir. During the patriotic performance, a military honor guard made a grand show of twirling their guns and firing blanks to punctuate the message that God is sending members of the religious right, in general, and the Christian Coalition, in particular, out to war.

Don Wildmon, president of the American Family Association, declared that "we are in the midst of a spiritual war" and the foundation of our country as well as the entirety of Western civilization is at stake. He characterized family breakdown, crime, pornography, and higher rates of abortion and divorce as symptoms of the spiritual war and volunteered himself as a soldier in the war.[128] Virginia Thomas, the committee liaison for Dick Armey, the Republican majority leader in the House of Representatives, believes that we must redraw the battle lines in our hearts and minds by reestablishing the centrality of God in our lives and in the wider society. She adds that this is necessary because of the power of the government, media, and the cultural elite, which is destroying the nation's very foundations.[129]

In 1993, Bill McCartney told attendees of a Promise Keepers conference in Boulder that he was calling them to war. He also told the clergy gathered at the Atlanta conference: "Many of you feel that you have been in a war for a long time. Yet the fiercest fighting is just ahead. God has brought us here to prepare us. Let's proceed. It's wartime!"[130] McCartney's pastor, James Ryle, noted that the only time 300,000 men have come together before is to wage war. His vision of Promise Keepers is one of freeing America from the evils of secularism, which he describes as "an abortion" of godliness.[131] Such use of imagery has been defended as being based in Scripture (specifically, 2 Cor. 10:3–5) and as, therefore, referring to spiritual warfare. The battle is purported to be between Jesus and the devil, heaven and hell. Furthermore, Promise Keepers defenders believe that, when dealing with men, using war- and sports-related imagery (especially when meeting in a football stadium) is natural.

It cannot be argued that using war and sports imagery is natural to organizations that are not made up exclusively of men. *Church and State* reported that at the 1993 Christian Coalition's

Annual Road to Victory Conference, attendees purchased T-shirts proclaiming "I Accelerate for Liberals" and "Nuke the Liberal Media." When asked to explain, a woman from the Illinois delegation explained that she often prays for the enemies of the Christian Coalition to die and defended such a sentiment as a biblical mandate: "We need to pray that they be converted or removed. It's very biblical."[132]

THE RELIGIOUS RIGHT AS A VICTIMIZED PEOPLE

A more recent aspect of the discourse of the religious right is the emphasis on how Christians are being victimized by a secular culture that is exceedingly hostile to their beliefs.

> As conservative Christians continue to lose ground in the great civil war of values, the cultural elites will continue their campaign to marginalize and paralyze us. They want to make it so uncomfortable for Christians to speak up, *even within their own denominations*, on issues of political correctness and public policy that they will cower in fear. They accomplish this not by dealing with the positions we take, but by name-calling and blatant disrespect. . . . Only Christians can be so marginalized.[133]

Ralph Reed, in his 1994 book, compared the contemporary treatment of religious people to the "separate sphere" once accorded women: that is, people of faith are "relegated to their churches and homes, where their faith poses no threat to the social order." Reed explained that the historical right to freedom *of* religion has been superseded by a secular emphasis on freedom *from* religion.[134]

Accusations of bigotry against Christians, which were common in Robertson's 1988 presidential campaign material, have increased in the last decade of the twentieth century. The purpose of some of the organizations of the religious right is to make the government more responsive to the issues raised by besieged pro-family Americans in general and evangelical Christians in particular. To no one's surprise, the Christian Coalition especially promotes the specter of Christians as an oppressed group: one of its main publications, the *Religious Rights Watch*, is dedicated solely to recording acts of discrimination against Christians. Its primary publication, *Christian American*, often carries accounts of anti-Christian bigotry. The charge is levied that anti-Christian bias is part of the strategy of the Democratic Party to dismiss Republicans. Robertson's 1993 book, *The Turning Tide*, has an appendix entitled "The War against Christianity," which is a recounting of "horror stories" of so-called anti-Christian bigotry run amok.[135]

The victim mentality was more than evident in a speech Pat Robertson gave at William and Mary Law School. He began by reciting the graphic details of the gang-rape of a teenage girl and then compared the crime to the rape of our society, in particular, the rape of "our nation's religious heritage, our national morality, of time-honored customs and institutions," committed at the hands of "liberal predators."[136] The religious right frequently compares the contemporary oppression of conservative Christians to the treatment of Jewish people in Hitler's Nazi Germany. Calls of alarm are relayed to spur good Christian people to take political action before the United States becomes as repressive as Nazi Germany. In a recent newsletter for Focus on the Family, James Dobson prayed that conservative Christians will have the courage of the Jewish people in Nazi Germany when the "severe adversity" that is sure to occur comes their way. Certainly, Dobson maintains, as society sinks further into the moral abyss, pro-family Christians will face ongoing intimidation.[137]

This victim mentality comes across especially in incidents where it is used as a defense for what might be construed as intolerant behavior. The *Washington Times* reported a case in which those opposing homosexuality were allegedly persecuted for their beliefs. A couple in Massachusetts were charged with violating the civil rights of their gay neighbor by displaying signs on their own porch that were derogatory in nature. A similar case involved employees reprimanded for voicing religious-based objections to attending a sensitivity-training workshop on homosexuality. Such charges, maintains the right, are proof that Christians, rather than lesbian women and gay men, are discriminated against.[138]

Gary Bauer, then president of the Family Research Council (and as of this writing on sabbatical to campaign for the Republican presidential nomination), in the midst of testimony on the De-

fense of Marriage Act, asserted that those who believe in traditional marriage were being discriminated against. He declared,
"It is not hatred to prefer normalcy. It is not bigotry to resist radical redefinition of marriage. It is not intolerance to believe in traditional morality."[139] More recently, he urged—in the political turmoil created by the July 1998 advertisements against homosexuality
—that Congress pass legislation in order to "prevent the federal
government from discriminating against people with traditional
views of sexual morality."[140]

Justin Watson, a religion scholar at Florida State University,
maintains that one of the key functions of claims to oppression is
"the moral clout that comes with victimhood." Because victimhood is so closely associated with the innocence of victims, it carries a moral force and, with it, claims to entitlement.[141] Claims to
victimhood provide an invaluable organizing tool: they motivate
conservative Christian voters to organize in the battle to defend
the innocence of good Christian families.

Where Is the Religious Right Going?

Bill McCartney, founder of the Promise Keepers movement, has
declared that, "by the year 2000, the strongest voice in America, a
booming voice, is going to belong to the men of God."[142] This
forecast, if it proves true, would be a dramatic turnaround from
just a generation ago. Fundamentalists have not always been participants in the political process because they viewed such participation as being contrary to the true Christian lifestyle.

In the ensuing decades, however, this sentiment has shifted. Ralph
Reed declared that citizenship is a "spiritual obligation" and urged
that Christians make their voices heard in the political arena.[143]
The ECWS also resolved to participate in the public debate about
values that are foundational to Christianity. Their recent "Christian Women's Declaration" makes clear the priority "to confront
the divisive and destructive forces" that undermine democracy.[144]

In his 1997 address to the Christian Coalition's annual Road to
Victory Conference, Pat Robertson congratulated the gathered
assembly on the progress made by the religious right: because of
their participation in the political process, their issues and con-

cerns were now the issues and concerns of the entire nation. Robertson declared that the goal of the pro-family movement was to bring back an America where "families are valued and children are cared for by two married heterosexual parents. . . . Where life is esteemed and valued from its earliest beginning to its final fading breath." The motivating factor of political involvement, he intoned, was a "desire to see our nation whole again."[145]

Ralph Reed describes the objective of the pro-family movement as one of participation instead of domination. By participating in the political arena, Reed maintains that pro-family Americans are trying to give their values, which he asserts are also the values of mainstream America, a voice.[146] When presenting the "Contract with the American Family," he attempted to reassure those who might be leery of legislating values and referred to the contract as the "ten suggestions, not the Ten Commandments." The goal, he claimed, was not to legislate family values, but to make sure "that Washington values families."[147] In this way the contract, Reed hoped, would be a start in the movement to shore up the family and restore traditional values. Earlier, however, Reed had expressed his plans for the Christian Coalition, commenting, "What Christians have got to do is to take back this country, one precinct at a time, one neighborhood at a time and one state at a time. . . . I honestly believe that in my lifetime we will see a country once again governed by Christians . . . and Christian values."[148] He reiterated the strategy at the 1998 Road to Victory Conference by highlighting the goal for the next decade of electing one hundred pro-life, pro-family candidates.[149]

When viewing the goals of the religious right, we see that involvement in political action is a phenomenon that is here to stay. No longer may conservative, pro-family Christians be justified in staying out of the political arena. As James Dobson urged in his June 1998 newsletter, "It is not enough to read the Bible. . . . Your concern and convictions must be translated into action."[150] The religious right cannot be dismissed easily. It is here for the long haul. The task before us is to formulate an analysis of its arguments. Who are we to do that? What are the assumptions we bring to the task? What does this religio-political battle have to do with our day-to-day lives?

PART 2

A Feminist Response

4

Whose Family? Whose Faith? What Justice?

Nothing short of a great Civil War of Values rages today throughout North America. . . . It is a war over ideas. And someday soon, [we] believe, a winner will emerge and the loser will fade from memory. But now, the outcome is much in doubt.[1]

James Dobson and Gary Bauer

As wonderful an institution as the family is, it can also be the place where people are everlastingly warped and doomed.[2]

Shirley and Pat Boone

The arguments of the religious right are an intricate web of theories, priorities, interpretations, perceived threats, and solutions parlayed with evangelical fervor. How can one attach a human face to this web, especially when one disagrees with it? In early October of 1997, I posed as a supportive wife and went to a prayer service sponsored by the Promise Keepers as part of its national rally in Washington, D.C.

One year later, during the last month of writing this book, I went to the annual Road to Victory Conference of the Christian Coalition. While I was there, I was regaled with speech after speech denouncing the Democratic president of the United States, uplifting Republican candidates, decrying abortion, and glorifying marriage between one man and one woman. I was the unsaved awash in a sea of fervent believers. I came away with more than faces to attach to the movement. I came away with a gut feeling that something, somewhere, is terribly wrong here in the Land of the Free. Many of the attendees felt the same way, but we felt the same way about different issues and for very different reasons. The gap was much larger than the one made by Charlton Heston (the banquet keynote speaker) parting the Red Sea. This new gap is one the world's best engineers cannot bridge.

Concerning the gap between liberal progressive folk and the religious right: There are no easy answers. There can be no reconciliation without justice. There can be no changing of their minds. There can be no true conversations/communication because the starting assumptions are not the same. The members of the religious right believe in a God who is judgmental, who will bring His (sic) wrath to bear on a town, like Orlando, the home of Walt Disney World, which dares to celebrate lesbian/gay pride, or on a nation, which they maintain has fallen into sin. They believe that men and women were born into proscribed gender roles. They believe that heterosexual, lifelong marriage is the only permissible context in which to express sexuality. They believe that poor people bring their poverty upon themselves and government has no duty toward them. They believe that America is a Christian nation.

I believe that God is a wildly inclusive God, who loves us fiercely.[3] I believe that God is a gentle, justice-loving God, who does not constrain human beings in a particular codified box. I believe that heterosexual, lifelong marriage is only one context in which one might express her or his sexuality. I believe that men and women are socially conditioned into believing that particular gender roles are proscribed. I believe that the United States is a nation of many faiths. I believe that, though poor people may be with us always, they are victims of late-twentieth-century monopoly capitalism, and the government must take responsibility for feeding, clothing, educating, and providing health care for all of its citizens.

So where shall the twain meet? They do not. Though perhaps they do in the sense that they and I have this in common: we are concerned about the condition of society—in particular, the condition of the family in contemporary society. I share some of the same concerns that those on the religious right voice. I, too, worry about the state of the family. I am concerned about what values our children are learning. I worry about the condition of the inner cities. I worry about the fact that so many intimate relationships are doomed to failure. However, even though I worry about these things, I do not worry about the same facets of these issues that the religious right does. I have neither the same assumptions about what the "threats" might be nor the same convictions about what the "solutions" are. In short, my sister and I may well be concerned about the same things, but we are concerned about them from different worldviews. The distance between us is, unfortunately, infinite, and yet in some ways it is not. We still hold things in common. We have in common that we care deeply for the same people. We have in common that we want to live in a safer world—for ourselves, our elders, and the next generation. We have in common that we—whether we like it or not—are family. And ultimately, that is what all of this is about.

Suspicions abound. Who has what to gain? What exactly is at stake here? In a time of uncertainty when people blame themselves for not achieving the American Dream and they are isolated, unaware of the wider implications of a late monopoly capitalist economy, when things are changing all around you and nothing is like it used to be, when the roles of men and women are in flux and you are confused about how to behave, when what you have always felt to be true about God and the Bible is being challenged by other people of faith as well as the wider society, when people are going bankrupt, your best friend is getting divorced, your son tells you he is gay, you discover your teenage daughter has had an abortion, and you get downsized from your job, what do you do?

We understand that when people are under stress and everything around them is changing, they want to hang on to what is familiar and what they believe brings comfort. We even understand that people like to look back at the past uncritically, remembering only the good things, and yearn for the uncomplicated past when men were men and women were women, when marriage meant one man and one woman (and no one thought to question it), when you knew no one being divorced, when you knew no one who was gay (and you thought "gay" meant "happy"), and when abortion was not even a blip on the radar screen. Back in those good old days, you could pretty much count on working for one company for thirty years. Back in those days, the words "God" and "country" were uttered in the same breath without fear of a lawsuit. Back in those days the American Dream still existed. Or at least we imagine it did.

Even though this yearning for the past, for when things seemed peaceful and comfortable, and life was simpler, is understandable, the nostalgic attempts to re-create the past today do not wash. They do not wash because society cannot be taken back to the days of yesteryear. They do not wash because yesteryear was not the way nostalgia recalls it. They do not wash because we no longer can afford to live out of a parochial worldview. Our worldview, of necessity, has become increasingly interconnected; it has become a global worldview, with many intertwining connections. No matter how much we want to hang on to the tried and true, the well worn and comfortable, we cannot do so in the same way we once did.

The religious right has a vested interest in maintaining the status quo, in maintaining the remembered norms of yesteryear. More specifically, a return to the safety net arena of the "traditional" family constellations is championed. So too are proscribed gender roles, and heterosexuality is definitely made compulsory. Beliefs about God are codified, frozen for all time; revelations of God are not ongoing. Family is narrowly defined, and those who do not fit the definition are summarily rejected. Acceptable ways of relating in marriage and other relationships are strictly laid out. Sexuality is firmly constrained. Norms for appropriate female behavior and male behavior are stubbornly maintained. Who has what to gain from all of this?

When society is in flux, when the smell of change is in the air, when chaos threatens to encroach on one's carefully guarded territory, human nature hangs on to the well-defined, familiar ways of being in this world. Those who have power struggle vigorously to hang on to it. Those who pose a threat to the power base are defined out of social institutions, such as family, marriage, and faith communities. This is a very effective ploy in the battle to hang on to the power and in the effort to comfort oneself in the midst of widespread change.

But let's look at what else may be at play here—fear. Elsewhere I have written about the effects of fear on those who do not have power, especially on those who have been abused.[4] Others besides the abused or the powerless are afraid as well. Those who have power are afraid of what life would be like if they lost their power and were no longer in control. Many on the religious right feel they are disempowered. They feel they are derided by the wider culture and are oppressed because of their Christian faith. They feel they are not taken seriously and are too often dismissed as being part of the fringe element. Suffice it to say that fear of losing their way of life motivates many of those on the religious right to involve themselves in the political struggle to save the family.

In a time rife with cultural crises and disruptions and characterized by growing uncertainty, fear abounds. With the ongoing nature of economic crisis in late-twentieth-century capitalism, triggered by increasing rates of dislocated workers and plummeting economies around the world, the fear is not likely to resolve itself soon. According to Christian social ethicist Marvin Ellison, in times of economic uncertainty, community disintegration and rising rates of social violence—such as hate crimes—occur. This is exacerbated by the fact that most people can no longer shape their own futures to the extent they would like and, indeed, lack the economic clout to support their families.[5] As a result of escalating panic, they fear the process of change that society is undergoing. They fear that their church, and thus their faith, is eroding. They fear for their marriages. They fear for the safety and moral well-being of their daughters and sons. They fear for the moral future of their country. They fear for the continuation of life-as-they-know-it. The factor of fear is a real part in shaping their arguments.

Today, when one enters the hallowed institution of marriage, one does so with the knowledge that as many as one in two marriages end up in divorce court. One can no longer count on the well-defined roles of the male as head of the household, protector of his family and property, and sole breadwinner. One can no longer assume that a woman will be content to sacrifice her career for that of her husband, stay at home with the children (assuming, of course, that a woman agrees to bear them in the first place), or submit to the leadership of her mate. Therefore, how does one know how to act? Add to this scenario the uncertainty that characterizes the world of work—that is, one can never be sure how long one will have employment—and the stage is set for a movement that would take us back to the good old days of *Father Knows Best*, when we thought all was well with the world, we knew what was expected of us, and we were safe.

I share the concerns of the religious right concerning the current condition of our families, society, and the world. Family life in this country—however it is defined—is on shaky ground. These days are perilous days indeed for the forming of families of whatever configuration as well as for the raising of children. The specters of domestic and street violence, rising rates of drug and alcohol abuse, the erosion of a safety net under the poorest of the poor, and deadly sexually transmitted diseases all make uncertainty and insecurity the rule rather than the exception. In addition, the economic pressures of day-to-day life have wreaked a toll on intimate relationships, disrupting the safe havens we call our homes and instilling a yearning for better times that the traditional family has come to represent. No one questions that our families are under siege. From this viewpoint, the appeal of "family values" and its concomitant promises of security and comfort are easy to understand.

Ralph Reed, in his 1994 book *Politically Incorrect*, paints a utopian picture, envisioning a world in which life is simpler, more carefree, without the trappings of a decadent contemporary culture that has strayed so far from the American tradition. In such a society, safe neighborhoods, strong schools, stable families, and lower taxes would be the order of the day:

> Government would be small because citizens and private institutions would voluntarily perform many of its functions. We would not need a large, bloated welfare state to take care of us, for we would take care of each other. We would not need the law to threaten or cajole us, for a higher law would live in our hearts. . . . Families would function again; marriages would work; children would be considered a blessing rather than a burden; neighbors would be neighbors again; government would be the servant instead of the master of a free and educated citizenry; revitalized communities would radiate from compassionate churches and

synagogues; and some of the most respected leaders in society would be pastors, priests, and rabbis. In short, we desire a good society based on the shared values of work, family, neighborhood, and faith.[6]

All of this can be had, maintains Reed, if conservative Christians are allowed to take their place as political and cultural leaders. With conservative Christians in leadership roles, America can, once again, be redeemed.

The difficulty with this idyllic scenario, however, is that the promises embedded in the value-laden rhetoric of family values are actually harmful rather than helpful to contemporary families. For instance, those on the religious right who maintain that lesbian and gay people are acceptable only if they seek out cures for their sexual orientation are harming families. As Sister Maureen Fiedler of the Quixote Center pointed out, such views encourage parents to reject their lesbian or gay children, forcing "them into self-rejecting counseling. It causes families to feel ashamed of sisters or brothers who are spoken of only in whispers. In some cases, it destroys family life itself, treating gay or lesbian children as outcasts."[7] The political rhetoric has fueled a vitriolic politics that, ironically, is eroding the social fabric upon which all of us depend. Motivated, in part, by a backlash against gains made in the area of civil rights for African Americans, women's equality, welfare benefits, and the acceptance of lesbian, gay, and bisexual people, family values discourse is rooted in fear and in anger against persons perceived to threaten the safe haven of the traditional family. That having been said, let's move now into an exploration of the theological assumptions underlying the arguments of the religious right.

As we have seen, those who are part of the religious right believe without question in the inerrancy of Scripture. This belief undergirds their insistence on a particular code of behavior that can be supported by the ultimate authority of Scripture. The Bible waving in evidence during the banquet entertainment for the Christian Coalition's 1998 Road to Victory Conference (which was alarming in combination with the militaristic display) was symbolic of the strong belief held in the God-given authority of Scripture—an authority that is, thus, above reproach and closed to any contrary arguments. This effectively cuts short all arguments from critics of the religious right and serves as the foundation for all of the political efforts the religious right undertakes in the name of the family.

Even at the beginning of the twentieth century, biblical literalism was an issue. As we recall from chapter 1, the fundamentalist movement was born in response to the new methods of biblical interpretation (namely, historical criticism) that were being taught in seminaries as well as the theory of evolution versus creationism. That has not changed over the years for conservative Christians. They maintain that the one way to read Scripture is through a literalistic lens. No concerns regarding historical and cultural contexts are entertained, and their own interpretations of Scripture are understood to be the only interpretations possible and are absolutized as God's voice. This one major assumption undergirds the theology of the religious right and is foundational to all other theological assumptions held.

Feminist liberation theologies, on the other hand, understand Scripture as one of many authoritative sources (along with reason, tradition, and especially the experiences of women and all oppressed people) for the doing of theology and the living of our lives.[8] Scripture is understood as being God-inspired and written by people. These two different points of view preclude any sort of agreement between the religious right and feminist liberation theologians from the start. Keeping that in mind, then, we turn to examine the theological assumptions regarding two doctrines—namely, those of creation and salvation—and their relation to the issues of gender roles, sexual orientation, marriage, and family.

BEING CREATED MALE AND FEMALE

Angie Warren, a twenty-two-year-old graduate student at Georgetown University, articulates what many women have felt for years: "They're calling for a return to traditional values, and it seems like it took us so long to get away from some of those values—like having one head of a family. Why can't women head it, too?"[9] But Pat Robertson speaks from a perspective that has held sway for eons: "As long as biology is what it is and women desire to mother children, the more sensible division of labor would be for the man to 'bring home the bacon' and the woman to 'fry it up in a pan.' But remember, only when they are together, male and female, can they be fruitful, fill the earth, and subdue it."[10] Through the theological lens of the doctrine of creation, we turn now to focus on the creation of humanity in two genders—male and female.

The creation of distinct male and female genders, along with the God-given roles for the genders, is a key tenet of the theology of the religious right. In terms of expectations for Christian behavior, this means that with the creation of two genders came the creation of a clear set of expectations regarding gender roles. These gender roles are seen as being willed by God. Each boy and girl is to grow up to marry a member of the opposite gender. Each man and woman is to understand the roles God has given him or her, embrace them enthusiastically, and refrain, as much as possible, from deviating from them. Deviation from proscribed gender roles is sin, which must be duly confessed and repented from. Although the advancement of women in the world of work may be accepted, albeit grudgingly (after all, working outside the home encourages "independence and self-sufficiency which God did not intend a married woman to have"),[11] women are ultimately expected to submit to the better judgment of their spouses. (Adam was commanded by God to rule the world. Evidently, that directive, as interpreted by the religious right, includes man ruling woman.) A woman is to desire more than anything the protection and honor associated with being married to a man. More important, she is to seek—as her one true vocation—the fulfillment of motherhood. These things are givens in the religious right's understanding of the creation of two genders.

The belief in female submission is derived from the belief in biological destiny as preordained by God. Woman's biological predisposition is to embrace the maternal vocation (which is assumed to make females in need of male protection), thus maintaining the subservient position of the biologically weaker gender. She is also to welcome gladly the leadership of her mate and submit to him regarding matters on which they disagree. Pat Robertson believes that women are happy to submit as long as their husbands love them.[12] Those women who are not enthusiastic about the prospect of being submissive are seen as adding to the general male confusion and insecurity about male gender roles, undermining the fragile male ego, and contributing to an entire nation of "sissified" men.[13] This, so the reasoning goes, ultimately results in the downward spiral of the nation. In effect, if woman is not part of the solution, she is part of the problem. "Godly women graciously submit to male spiritual headship."[14] Women who are truly feminine live to build up the family, do not appropriate masculine characteristics, and gladly leave the leadership role to their men. In this way, the two genders complement each other.

Recently, a new focus on fatherhood has emerged. David Blankenhorn's work on fatherlessness through the National Fatherhood Initiative (admittedly, a more centrist organization) seeks to make responsible fathers a nationwide priority.[15] Groups such as the Promise Keepers and the 1995 African American Million Man March have shifted public attention away from motherless children to fatherless children. Fatherlessness has been blamed for the rise of school dropout rates, early sexual activity among teenagers, drug and alcohol abuse, and the rising number of episodes of violence experienced or perpetrated by children. While we see the importance of upholding male responsibility to children and admire the fact that more men are beginning to take their responsibilities seriously, we also see that the new fatherhood movement, along with its compatriots on the religious right, too often blames women in general and feminists in particular for the absence of male figures in children's lives. As sociologist Judith Stacey notes, it is past time for men to realize that they need to become more involved with their children; however, all too often women are blamed for having expectations that are too high regarding male involvement in family affairs and are thus accused of frightening their men away. At the other end of the spectrum, women are blamed for turning down male participation in parenting.[16] This phenomenon speaks volumes about the contradictory and complicated issue of male gender involvement in matters of the home. It also reveals a deep-seated ambivalence regarding the involvement of men with their children—a reluctance to participate in a traditionally female bastion.

If deliberate deviation from God-ordained gender roles is sinful, then feminism—which dares to question what has been deemed to be unquestionable—is the harbinger of familial and societal destruction. Reinforced by the analysis that gender roles are cultural constructs, feminists dare to question the doctrine known as biological destiny: creation. With their advocacy of "sinful behavior patterns,"[17] feminists dare to challenge the age-old pattern of family life and marital relationships, contradicting "biblically-based faith and time-tested moral behavior."[18] With their pioneering work into inclusive liturgies and ritual, feminist liberation theologians dare to re-imagine God. Thus, feminists have been branded heretical and blamed with creating "a place of profound disorder" in American families.[19]

So feminism begins to ask the hitherto unaskable questions and braves new ways of seeing social institutions. Using the tools given us by feminist liberation theology, I raise the following questions:[20] Why should the creation of two distinct genders automatically mean that men and women should therefore have distinct social roles based on gender differences? Who has what to gain and what is at stake in this division of gender roles? Where is the power, and who wants to hold on to it? The complementarity theory—which posits that female and male natures "fit together"—is a foundational part of conservative Christian reasoning and is the entire underpinning of the arguments for female submission and male headship.[21] But feminist liberation theologians question the necessity for female submission and male headship and debunk the complementarity theory.

The complementarity theory is understood to be the foundation of efforts to control women, sexuality, and the sacred institution of marriage. The effect of such a theory is to control the entire realm of human relationships, beginning with male/female relationships and extending, by mandate, to relationships that encompass entire families, communities, and ultimately, the nation. This control is ideological in nature and effectively dismantles any opposition argument by pointing to the authority of the Bible. Since the Bible is seen as the ultimate authority, which by definition cannot be questioned, that effectively stops short any challenge. Nevertheless, feminists who view biblical authority as being only one among a number of sources of authority question why relationships must be confined to a heterosexual model. If our God is a God of love rather than judgment (an assumption not necessarily shared with those on the religious right), then the most important thing is not who we love and under what circumstances, but that we love. (Note: this is not meant to imply that single people fall short by not being coupled; rather, it is meant to affirm the reality of different family formulations, such as various extended families, close friends one might consider "family," and our animal companions.) Constraining gender relations and expectations to only one scenario sets up failure from the beginning. So too with family formation.

In terms of gender roles, feminist liberation theology pushes open what is considered normative for human beings as we actually live and serves as a reality check. How many family homes back in the good old days of yesteryear were actually happier places than those of today? How free from dissent, violence, and economic woes were families of the past that are so longed for? Was the family hearth really as peaceful and as safe a haven as we remember? If so, for whom?

When we look back at our family histories (those of us who are old enough, that is), we can begin to raise the questions of what the family dynamics were at the time. If, for instance, we are nostalgic for the father-knows-best family life of the 1950s, are we guilty of remembering only the good things? Have we filtered out the conflict? Do we know that our mothers were fulfilled by staying at home (that is, those of us who were privileged enough to have mothers who could afford to stay at home)? How did they feel about giving up those "Rosie the Riveter"–type jobs they held during World War II? Were they happy to turn their jobs over to the men returning home from war? What were those times like for women who had to work, not only during the war, but before and after it? What was it like for women who took care of other people's homes and other people's children, who cooked other people's meals and cleaned other people's houses? For those who could stay home, did one salary adequately cover the economic needs of the household? What did the woman do whose husband beat her up? What did the child do who was sexually molested in his or her home? Was everyone as happy as our nostalgia would tell us? What about the threats to family and social life that loomed on the horizon—the Korean War, the Red Menace, the McCarthy era? Didn't folks feel that their society was spiraling out of control? Were they not concerned about the safety of their families? Did they, too, yearn for the good old days of yesteryear?

Perhaps if we can begin to speak honestly of our family stories, we will see that the idyllic picture of the past we held has its own share of concerns, turmoil, and uncertainties. Perhaps we can see that even back in the good old days, people—especially white women living in the houses with those infamous white picket fences—were lonely and yearned for something beyond their perfect, happy families. Perhaps, occasionally, the facade would crack, and a woman would wonder what the world would be like if she were free to explore her untapped potential.

Members of the religious right offer a palliative to the social and political chaos in contemporary U.S. society: they offer an idyllic vision of a peaceful, harmonious past that never really existed. The all-too-brief post–World War II boom created an economic climate in which jobs were plentiful, housing was affordable, and after the horrors of fighting a world war, all seemed stable and in good order—at least for white people. This time period is romanticized as a time when traditional family values were embraced by all and when America was truly an upstanding Christian nation, rewarded by God for its faith. What is glossed over, however, is the fact that this time of stability, good order, and true family values was also a time of segregation and racist violence, illegal abortions resulting in the tragic deaths of women, and the keeping of family secrets such as battering, incest, rape, and alcoholism. It was a time when the corporate world was experiencing rapid growth, and the traditional nuclear family was being wrenched from its network of extended family. It was a time when lesbian women and gay men were invisible and isolated, and when they were discovered, they were threatened with incarceration in mental hospitals, public disclosure, and /or violence against their persons. It was a time when people had to be white to enjoy any of the benefits of those glorious days of yesteryear to which so many among us so desperately wish we could return.

In the same way that gender roles are constrained by the religious right, so too are issues of who can love whom and under what circumstances. There can be no deeper challenge to biologically determined gender roles than the existence of those who prefer to be in intimate relationship with a member of their own gender. Such a reality undermines every theory posited about gender complementarity and biological determinism and threatens, to the core, conservative theological doctrine on the creation of two genders.

No wonder, then, generally speaking, issues affecting lesbian, gay, and bisexual people serve as lightning rods for the vitriolic rhetoric of the religious right. Conservative Christians understand the so-called homosexual agenda to have a deleterious moral impact on the well-being of the family, society as a whole, and the entire nation, which would invite divine retribution. Viewing it through a lens that, at best, interprets homosexuality as a disease that can be cured (but only if the victim first repents), the religious right argues that, unchecked, homosexual behavior poses a danger to America's families and communities. Furthermore, homosexuality is considered to be in violation of God's plans for the human race, runs counter to biblical law as laid out in the Genesis account of creation, and has the potential to devastate American culture.[22] Heterosexism and homophobia are thus justified both theologically and biologically.

Homosexuals who fail to repent from their sins are deemed a threat to children, to the family, and to the country. Homosexuality is pronounced to be seriously antifamily. Those who identify as lesbian, gay, or bisexual have to contend with the fact that they, by virtue of their identities, are defined out of the family. They are deemed unacceptable citizens in society at large. This reaction was clearly at work during the Christian Coalition's 1998 Road to Victory Conference when I, along with two friends who attended, placed a rainbow sticker on my name tag. The first indication that I was "unacceptable" came when I was trying to get in line for the banquet dinner. Upon spying my rainbow-decorated name tag, one woman said to her companion, "What is a homosexual doing in here?" Feeling more than slightly like I was in the belly of the beast, I entered the banquet hall only to be accosted by a man who waved his finger in my face and belligerently told me that I, as a "homosexual," had no right to be there. I then removed my name badge so that I could do my research unimpeded and also, quite frankly, so that I would feel safer. These two incidents were relatively minor on the continuum of harassment of lesbian/gay people, but they illustrate well the extent to which lesbian, gay, and bisexual people are viewed as anathema by those on the religious right.

Not only does the individual lesbian or gay person, in the eyes of the religious right, pose a threat, but the idea that two women or two men would want to—and this is key—*live together in a home like a married couple and maybe even raise children* is threatening also. This specter leads conservative Christian opponents of such ideas to run for their Bibles and the safe shores of tradition, claiming sovereignty for the sacred, God-ordained institution of heterosexual marriage. Even centrists such as David Blankenhorn explicitly denounce lesbian child-rearing, insisting that in a decent society, people do not involve themselves "in the production of radically fatherless children."[23] Such statements support in a dangerous way the agenda of the religious right.

In the name of defending heterosexual marriage, much hateful rhetoric and many hate-filled acts spew forth from the mouths and hands of those who invoke God's name. In the name of defending the assertion that only a man and a woman can fall in love, same-gender love is vilified. The murder in October 1998 of Matthew Shepard, a freshman at the University of Wyoming, because he was gay, is gruesome evidence of this. In the name of the traditional family, many other configurations of family are denounced, defiled, and dismissed. To make matters worse, the current climate of homophobic backlash is causing some liberal leaders in our churches to back off from their defense of lesbian and gay people. Lesbian and gay folks who seek support from their spiritual leaders are more and more being told to be subtle, to stop talking about the details of their lives, and to return to the closet because the times in which we live are too dangerous. Dangerous for whom? They have always been dangerous for lesbian and gay people. Are times too dangerous for our white, heterosexual, liberal supporters? Do they have to put too much on the line to continue their stand for justice? Are they prepared to go only so far? What exactly is at stake and for whom? Just who is standing on the line? Why does this problem exist in the first place?

The subject is overcomplicated. Why does who loves whom matter? What is the difference whether I commit myself to a man or to another woman? Is not our loving—and loving well—more important? Would God really disown children who sought to love justly? Something is dreadfully askew here. In a social order in which we are concerned about children dying from stray bullets, rising rates of drug and alcohol abuse, and increasing levels of violence in our homes and on the streets, why in the world are we wasting precious time on arguing about who can love whom and in what ways?

The possibility of legitimate, loving, God-blessed relationships between two women or two men must really appear frightening to those who hold dear to their hearts the ideal of the traditional family. Such possibility raises many questions and possesses the potential of toppling that house of cards known as "family values." If such relationships are not damned by God, if women do not necessarily need men to be happy and fulfilled, if happy families can exist who are not of the traditional type, if two men can be tender and passionate with each other, if a relationship between two men or two women is an example to the rest of the community of devotion and passion, if the children raised in lesbian or gay families turn out to be "normal," well, what then? What does that mean for the assumptions on which the adherents of the religious right have based their family values? What does it mean for the way they have ordered the universe? What does it mean for their understanding of God, family, and loving?

Social ethicist Marvin Ellison writes about the phenomenon of moral panics, which are especially prevalent during times of great social change. The traditional structures of marriage and family will never cease to exist, yet the religious right focuses on this fear in times of stress and change. Ellison notes that this common pattern has occurred throughout history:

> During the 1880s, with the massive social disruptions caused by urban industrialization, moral crusades were launched to stop vice.

Purity campaigns, largely aimed at bolstering middle-class influence with immigrants and the working poor, sought to outlaw prostitution and end the practice of masturbation. During the 1950s, at the height of the Cold War, social fears about communism focused on the "homosexual menace" and juvenile delinquency. In our own tumultuous time, welfare recipients, urban (black) youth, feminists, and gay/lesbian/bisexual people are the targets of right-wing attack.[24]

Ellison's description of moral panics is key to considering the dynamics at work around issues of family. When a great deal of change occurs in a particular society, sexuality is almost always at the root of the moral panic. One can argue that the subject of a moral panic serves the interests of those in power well: it detracts attention from more serious issues of racism and economic decline. Note, for instance, in today's climate, the public focus has been on the sexual misdeeds of President Bill Clinton and the purging of homosexuality from U.S. society rather than on the deteriorating state of the global economy, the human casualties from the dismantling of welfare, the addressing of racism, or the impending Y2K crisis. The bottom-line issue is power—or the ideology of control. Those who seek to keep the two genders in tightly constrained roles and lesbian/gay/bisexual people from being seen as upstanding citizens are trying desperately to hang on to the power to define moral reality.[25] Those who do not fit within the proscribed model pose a threat to authority and social order; they undermine the traditional family and fly in the face of patriarchal authority. No wonder, then, that those who seek to maintain traditional family values respond so judgmentally to those who refuse to conform. As Ellison reminds us, maintaining patriarchal authority demands limiting sexual behavior to "male-controlled heterosexual marriage."[26] The survival of the American Dream, of the possibility of return to the good old days of yesteryear, demands it.

The doctrine of the creation of two distinct genders is challenged here by the possibility that two people of the same gender could love each other legitimately. When viewing the doctrine from a lens of feminist liberation theology, we must query what power, if any, this doctrine has over our lives. How does the doctrine of the creation of two genders enhance our lives? How is it life-giving? To whom is it life-giving? Is it life-giving at the expense of others? Who benefits by it? Who is marginalized by it? This doctrine should not be thrown out with the bath water. To the contrary, seeing how it might be interpreted from a justice-centered standpoint is important. A doctrine of the creation of two genders is a wonderful blessing in that it provides different human experiences. With difference exists the possibility of learning from the other's experience. With difference comes a variety of ways of experiencing the physical world. When these gender differences are exploited to control the other or to make one who is perceived to be less powerful submit to the other, such doctrinal rigidity feeds an ideology of control and fuels moral panics.

Along with gender differences comes the possibility of lesbian, gay, bisexual, and heterosexual relationships. If any one of the relationships is deemed normative, and all relationships are supposed to conform to those standards, then the doctrine of creation needs to be challenged. A feminist liberation theological gaze sees the doctrine of creation of two genders as opening up a myriad of possibilities for relationships. This doctrine can be celebrated as opening up models of relationship, not closing down the art of human relationality to one legitimate model. Human relationships between and among the genders must be about upholding justice and love, not about maintaining control. A feminist liberation theo-ethical hermeneutic insists on a model of relationship that incorporates the particularities and practicalities of our lives as we actually live them; it is not based on a nostalgic longing for the ideal family of yesteryear. Perhaps, dare I suggest, that ideal never really existed in the way that we remember it.

SALVATION BY MARRIAGE AND FAMILY

The salvation of America from the ravages of gender role confusion and same-sex liaisons can come only from shoring up the traditional bastions of (heterosexual) marriage and conventional (man plus woman plus children) families. Or so the religious right tells us. The challenge that liberals, feminists, and lesbian/gay/

bisexual people have posed to rigidly defined gender roles and traditional male-female relationships has set off alarm bells for those who hold that gender identity and sexuality are preordained by God. The only way to maintain control, to safeguard families, indeed, to save the soul of America, is to shore up the defenses around the sacred institution of marriage and the traditional family structure.

The possibility of marriages other than those between one man and one woman has exacerbated the moral panic around issues of sexuality. One argument against same-gender marriage is that such unions would lead to marriages between three people or between an adult and a child or between blood relatives. Another is that it violates God's law. If same-gender marriages were to take place, one doomsayer foretold that the "institution of marriage, as we know it, created by God, will come to an end throughout the world in six months to one year!"[27] Alan Keyes, at the Christian Coalition's 1998 Road to Victory Conference, attacked the "radical homosexual agenda that assaults every idea of family responsibility, fidelity, and integrity." The support of such an agenda only abandons the "basic principles of justice on which this nation was founded and on which its strength depends."[28]

The level of moral panic has reached new heights. Since marriage is considered to be the very foundation of what defines the country both in individual and in cultural terms, the religious right has mounted an extensive campaign to defend that foundation as both a religious duty and a civic duty. If the exclusive club of marriage is considered to be under attack, then those who seek to defend that exclusivity will pull out all the stops, postulating that the institution of marriage is endangered, connecting the survival of traditional marriage to the stability of society, claiming that marriage has always been the basic building block of civilization, and entwining the salvation of the nation (sometimes described as God's continued blessing of the country with favored nation status) with the continued definition of marriage as a lifelong covenant between one man and one woman. Thus, the argument for protecting traditional marriage (while excluding the possibility of same-gender marriages) is based on appeals to ensuring the best interest of family members, future generations, the church, the entire social order, and the nation. The end result is that conventional sexual ethics is formulated on maintaining controls over sexuality that could become aberrant at any time—that is, sex can be considered good only if it takes place between one man and one woman in the context of divinely ordained heterosexual marriage. An even better goal of that sex is to reproduce the human race. (This despite Patrick Fagan's suggestion that the only way to save the nation is for good Christian folk to consider abstinence within marriage!)[29]

The religious right argues that the fact that society has meandered away from the idea that heterosexual marriage is the sole acceptable way of being in intimate relationship has led to a rise in the incidence of widespread social problems, which threaten the survival of the nation. Advocates of traditional marriage as the only acceptable form of relationship tout it as the only way to keep social problems under control. Indeed, some even claim that marriage leads "to more fulfilled and even longer lives."[30] To go against what God has ordained and what our God-created biology has imprinted in our natures is to court societal, national, and theological disaster. Only by bestowing a special protection on traditional marriage—and reserving that special protection for sacred unions between one man and one woman—can we have any hope of saving ourselves, the nation, and ultimately, the world.

In postulating that our salvation is tied in to keeping the benefits of marriage limited to unions consisting of one man and one woman, the religious right's agenda of control is clear. The power and privilege reserved for such unions are not to be tampered with, lest an angry God wreak vengeance on a disobedient population. Too much is at stake here. The centuries-old connection of marriage with property, and more specifically with male property rights in a capitalist ethos, has filtered down into present-day discourse on the sanctity of heterosexual marriage. This cannot be dismissed lightly. Ellison observes,

> In a capitalist patriarchy, men exercise the right of property ownership, especially over female partners. The fiction of a scarcity of love further justifies competition for establishing monopoly control over another person as one's personal "supply." Capitalist ide-

ology also reinforces the prevailing antisexual, erotophobic ideology by positing that the desire for pleasure leads inexorably to narcissistic self-indulgence.[31]

The equation of marriage with property ownership is reflected in the emphasis on male headship and female submission. The effect of defending male headship and female submission by maintaining that such power relations are ordained by God in the Genesis accounts of creation lays the groundwork for connecting male/female power relations with an ethos of property ownership. Feminist scholar Carole Bohn describes this as propagating a "theology of ownership," which, in turn, is used to justify social norms of unequal male/female gender relations.[32] This theology of ownership has been foundational to Christianity throughout the centuries and is evident in the contemporary emphasis of religious right groups on male headship and female submission: those who are the heads exercise dominion. This ownership is also present in the defense of marriage as a God-ordained, sacred institution. Unfortunately, this theology is dangerous stuff indeed. It shores up unequal gender relations and has the effect of turning a blind eye to the violence that takes place within the sacred institution of marriage. Bohn notes the messages that such a theology sends, especially when abused women have desperately sought advice from their conservative pastors:

> Marriage is sacred and you must do whatever you can to hold it together. Your husband is the head of your household; do what he tells you and he won't need to resort to violence. You must have done something to provoke him; go home and mend your ways so he will not need to behave in this manner. All of us must suffer; it makes us more Christ-like. Offer up your suffering to Jesus and he will give you strength to endure.[33]

Violence is a symptom of the theology of ownership; it is a tool used to control, to maintain order. The incidence of violence rises when the status quo of that control is threatened. The theology of ownership—the insistence on male headship and female submission, no matter how sugarcoated it may be—ultimately feeds into an ideology of control. The insistence of the sacredness of only one form of relationship—that of lifelong marriage between one man and one woman—bespeaks the desire to maintain control over relationships, sexuality, and women.

Cloaked in the guise of the good of the family, of Christianity, of the social order, of the nation, the insistence of the religious right on defending one form of relationship over all others is about holding on to the power to define our singular reality. If one has the power to define (such as God gave Adam), then one has control; indeed, one has God's blessing. God as the Holy Other defines us. Adam—the male of the species, made in the image of God and appointed by God to have dominion—defines women and the appropriate context for male-female relationships. Thus, only those who conform to the model of lifelong, one man plus one woman marriage are valid. Those who deviate from that definition "fall short of the glory of God, the true nature that is designed for us by God," and "are that much less than fully human."[34]

The romanticization of marriage shores up the belief that traditional marriage is the only acceptable form of relationship. Beginning in the Victorian era, the cult of true womanhood, otherwise known as the cult of domesticity, grew in popularity, primarily as a result of the industrial revolution, which made it possible for a woman to run the household and for the man of the house to earn enough money to support his household. A clearer division of gender roles emerged and was justified by the appeal to male headship. This romantic understanding of the nature of marriage resulted in propagating the myth that there is one, and only one, person of the opposite gender who is meant for each of us. This person is to fulfill all the longings one has ever had and complements and completes one. This supports the infrastructure of traditional marriage by upholding its predestined, preordained nature. It also fosters a dependency that encourages us to look to our mates to fill all of our needs, thus isolating us from friends and family.

Feminist and pro-feminist theologians have long insisted the time has come to discard those highly romanticized understandings of marriage. Such understandings only propagate a theology of ownership and reinforce an ideology of control. Such understandings mark the institution of marriage as one that fosters exclusion rather than inclusion, law rather than spirit.

Those who romanticize heterosexual marriage advocate the deliberate refusal to recognize more than one legitimate reality. The religious right is aware of other realities, but the religious right is struggling against the existence of other realities of relationship. If those of the religious right recognized other forms of relationship to be as legitimate and blessed by God as traditional marriage, then they would lose control and, from their point of view, would lose the struggle to save the country. It is as simple as that: the salvation of the nation is at stake!

This huge gulf cannot be bridged unless one side gives in totally to the other. A feminist liberation theology honors deeply the diversity among us. It recognizes a reality that encompasses and honors the different lived experiences of relation. When contemporary society has tolerated sexual activity outside marriage (of the heterosexual sort), it has usually done so because it has been understood that such activity leads to marriage. This tolerance is a false tolerance and effectively undergirds the status quo. In the meantime, both the perspective of the religious right and the liberal point of view fail to take into account the existence of single people who are perfectly happy not being in a "coupled" relationship and gay/lesbian/bisexual people whose relationships are labeled "promiscuous." The class and race bias is evident as assumptions are made about the white and middle-class background of those whose realities are described as being normative. Thus, as social ethicist Mary Hobgood reminds us, the only relationships considered to be of any worth in a social order that understands traditional marriage as normative are those that are both heterosexual and monogamous.[35]

THE TRADITIONAL FAMILY AS SALVATION

The traditional family, which issues forth from the sacred union of one man plus one woman, is the cornerstone of human society—or so claims the religious right. Midge Decter of the Heritage Foundation has stated, "What is it Mother Nature knows that so many of us no longer do? It is that marriage and family are not a choice like, say, deciding where to go and whom to befriend and how to make a living. Together, marriage and parenthood are the rock on which human existence stands."[36]

This male-female coupling is guarded carefully as the only true form of family that will save the nation from the brink of moral disaster. To fail to nurture the well-being of the traditional family risks the futures of women and children and, according to Pat Robertson, is an abdication of our responsibilities as citizens: as the family goes, so goes the nation.[37] As we have seen, the deterioration of the traditional family is understood by the religious right to be the single greatest threat to the future of good, God-fearing Americans.

The traditional form of family—the nuclear family—is understood, like traditional marriage, to be God ordained. The family is the place where, no matter what is going on in the world, all is well. It is a place of nurture, solace, and safety. People cling to this notion of family for all they are worth. Those who believe that this is the one true way of being family are prepared to fight to the death to protect it. Many literally mean that. The family is the source of salvation for a weary, embattled, and disheveled world. If all can be made right with the family, all will be made right with the world. On this foundational notion, the religious right pins all its hope. Midge Decter asked while lecturing on the topic of family: "How did we as a society ever come to this disordered place?"[38] How, indeed? Something primal and deep within us beckons to these calls for tradition, family, and safe havens.

The traditional family is, in actuality, not all that traditional and is a modern concept that many on the Christian right mistakenly believe is "an ancient, essential, and now-endangered institution."[39] Historically, the "Roman familia referred to all that which belonged to the paterfamilias, including slaves and servants, as well as relatives by blood or marriage." According to the *Oxford English Dictionary*, the first usage of the term "family" did not occur until around the beginning of the fifteenth century, at which point it indicated the servants of a particular household.[40] During this era, many families could not afford to raise their own children, and offspring were often apprenticed, sold, or sent to a convent or monastery. Not until the late seventeenth century did the contemporary meaning of family—as "the group of persons consisting of the parents and their children, whether actually living together or not"—come into popular usage.[41] Most living in that period understood that marriage was not possible for many people; people generally anticipated that some would not be able to reside with their biological families.

Not until the Victorian era, in the mid-nineteenth century, did our understanding of the term "family" come into general practice. That was possible only because of the advances of the industrial revolution and the rise of the middle class. Thus, those on the religious right who believe that the traditional family has been biblically mandated and sanctioned by society throughout the centuries have failed to read their history. Family life, as we have come to understand it, has not been practiced until relatively recently. The traditional family is a form of family life connected with the existence of the middle class and, more particularly, with the rise of a white middle class. The industrial revolution in the mid-nineteenth century separated, for the first time, paid work from the household. A man was considered a success if he could afford to be the sole breadwinner and for the "lady of the house" to be just that. This form of family life became so connected with the idea of "family" that the labor movement fought for decades to achieve a living wage for the male breadwinner. The majority of working white American males achieved this piece of the American Dream only after World War II.[42]

The story of family life was much different for African Americans. Battered by the death-giving practices of slavery, family life—as defined by the religious right—was virtually impossible. Southern slave owners in the early nineteenth century encouraged slaves to form families; they did so motivated by the knowledge that allowing slaves to develop family ties would discourage organized rebellions and attempts to escape. Families would also reproduce the labor pool. Thus, slave families were allowed to form in order to benefit the white slavocracy. The forming of family units by no means implied that all was well. Those living under the conditions of slavery were subject to a benevolent master who had to be kept mollified. Transgressions could result in members of slave families being sold and the maiming or deaths of those who dared to challenge the system. Women were vulnerable to rape at the hands of their seemingly benevolent masters, regardless of whether they had formed family ties (slaves were prohibited from marrying legally and had no right to shape the course of their children's lives). Slave women, after all, were considered property—as were the African American men in their lives—and thus were seen as less than human and as objects to be used. Many bore children conceived out of rape by their white slave masters. Those white slaveowners who defended the institution of slavery claimed that any change in the status of the enslaved would result in the downfall of the economic system maintained by slavery, the institution of the family, and society as a whole.[43]

After emancipation, dislocated African Americans floundered in search of economic survival. In the late nineteenth and early twentieth centuries the migration of African Americans to the cities of the North and South resulted in further economic dislocation. This migration, coupled with the overtly expressed racial hostility that had flourished since the ending of the Civil War, worked against the African American family. Threatened by violence and poverty, families were hard-pressed to survive. With the advent of the world wars, many African Americans gained economically only to be downsized out of their jobs when white men returned from war.

The American Dream proved elusive to African American families. While increasing numbers of white families were able to achieve the so-called traditional family format of the male breadwinner and the stay-at-home housewife, this ideal proved to be unattainable for many African Americans. Instead of staying at home to see to their own households and their own children, African American women, from economic necessity, had to work outside the home—often taking care of white people's households and children; their participation in the workforce, at a cheaper wage, shored up the white American Family Dream while simultaneously chipping away at African American family life.

Because of the violent history of racism in this country, the ideal of family life is not equally applicable to all groups of people. When the icon of the family is held up, we must ask: To whose family are we referring? Just how traditional is the family? Whose values are we upholding? And when nostalgic refrains for the return to the good old days of family life fill the air, we must query, How good were those days? For whom? For white women? For white children? For African American women? For African American children? For African American men? Did those good old days actually exist? Or do they exist only in our belief that surely the days of yesteryear had to be better compared to the uncertain times in which we now find ourselves?

Families—contemporary ones and those of yesteryear—are all too often not the safe havens that their defenders would have us believe. As Shirley and Pat Boone (in their quote at the beginning of this chapter) noted, families "can also be the place where people are everlastingly warped and doomed."[44] The violence that women and children across all economic and race backgrounds experience is extensive. The violence that takes place in our homes is rooted in the theology of ownership that undergirds the mandate of male headship and female submission. Seeing women and children as property imbues them with nonperson status; when property is granted nonperson status, the owner has no compunctions about using physical violence to keep nonpeople in line. When relationships between men and women are defined on the basis of male subordination and female submission, when gender differences are constructed as the superiority of one gender over another, and when gender-based distinctions are justified as being "natural" and God ordained, violence against women and children flourishes. Such justifications of violence filter into popular culture, and violence is thus understood as "the means by which men can stay in control or regain control over 'their' women" and children.[45] The family, far from being a haven from a heartless world, becomes all too often for women and children a battleground upon which male authority is defended. In such a climate, the ideology of control is alive and well.

The religious right is correct in its estimation that feminism poses a threat to the traditional family of yesteryear. The changes that have occurred in the latter half of the twentieth century in terms of women's inroads into the world of work and the questioning of the extent to which biology is destiny have threatened those who wish to turn back the clock to a happier time, when women were women and men were men, a man's home was his castle, and no one was confused over gender identity issues. The religious right, as the champion of a social order that, in actuality, existed for only a brief period of time, fuels the angst of those disturbed over a changing social milieu. As levels of frustration and desperation rise over the state of contemporary society, so do levels of violence. The ideology of control is shored up. As feminist theologian Karen Bloomquist observes, control over women "must be maintained *at any cost* because it is the core moral value that generates males' sense of identity and worth in this society. . . . Violence is a way to keep control, to maintain your identity."[46] She continues,

> The threat of the male prerogative being given up or taken away evokes in men panic and a feeling of impending chaos that may result in a violent reaction. Those women with whom such a man is in close relationship become the most likely targets of violence, be it physical, mental, or spiritual. Such violence is a response to what is sensed to be the destruction of previously absolute, actually unjust, social structures. Whether the social order has really changed that much, whether many women actually do find themselves in positions with public power is not the issue. What is important is the public rhetoric that asserts that to be the case.[47]

For many people faced with the specter of changing gender roles and the perceived disintegration of the traditional family, a panic—more accurately, a *moral* panic—ensues. The mounting backlash is palpable. Threatened with change, more specifically, the changing face of the American family, the religious right is morally panicked over the loss of a highly controlled, highly idealized, and highly defined family context. Although no organization that we have examined in these pages would ever publicly champion violence as a way to hang on to control (many expressly disapprove of male tendencies to resort to violence against women and children), the effect of a theology of ownership, an ideology of control, and the practice of male headship (no matter how benevolent it might prove to be) and female submission is to undergird violence as a way to maintain control. The state of moral panic among the religious right regarding the traditional family as the way to personal and national salvation heightens this effect even more.

A more subtle, yet effective, form of control employed by the religious right consists of accusations of immorality and charges of violating the sacred interests of good Christian family life. This is an especially virulent form of control present both in the political arena and in the sphere of denominational politics; the result: to induce a moral panic that compromises the ability of liberal church leaders and politicians to focus on substantive matters of church and state.

What some call a theology of ownership, what others call domination politics,[48] and what I have referred to as an ideology of control is based on the belief that one type of person (male, heterosexual, white, or wealthy) is superior to another type of person (female, lesbian or gay, African American, Hispanic, Asian, American Indian, and/or poor). In terms of social structures, marriage between one woman and one man is valued as the one and only morally acceptable way of being in an intimate relationship. In a similar fashion, the protection of the so-called traditional family, and the exclusion of all other groupings that would be called family, is seen as being the superior and only way of saving the entire social order from divine judgment. In the name of salvation, the traditional family and the longed-for days of yesteryear are held up as the solution to the problems ailing contemporary society. The battle for the soul of the nation hinges no less on the restoration of the traditional family structure—and with it, traditional marriage—as the sole normative, morally acceptable option for upstanding Christians.

Even those who have declared a culture war in order to defend family values cannot seem to integrate the importance of families into their own lives. Former Speaker of the House Newt Gingrich, upon taking office, vowed to restructure the mad-pace congressional work schedule because it "brutalizes and damages families." Yet he held the 1995 Congress over into the Christmas recess during a partisan-induced gridlock with President Clinton. Despite his intentions to initiate a more humane workload on Congress, the work schedule became so intrusive to family time under his leadership that one Republican congressman claimed that he and his colleagues had resorted to raising their "children by memo," and that, within the conservative freshman congressional class of 1995, marriages quickly began to fall apart.[49]

What are we to make of this? While Gingrich's inability to follow through on his family values intentions is striking for the inconsistencies it reveals, I suspect that this sort of ambivalence is common. Indeed, to be fair, even those of us who find Gingrich's political proclivities to be abhorrent (if not downright dangerous) are not immune from failing to follow through with practices that would make our lives, and those of our colleagues, more manageable, family-friendly, and sensible. Having said that, I believe that the religious right is guilty of romanticizing the cozy return to the good, old-fashioned family values scenario. Gingrich's indiscretion is symptomatic of this tendency. The fact remains that the appeal to defend traditional marriage against the threat of other loving relationships and the intent to exclude all whose families do not conform to the traditional definition of "family" from using that term (and thus reaping the sociopolitical and spiritual benefits due those who conform to "marriage" and "family" definitions) are not based in reality. The reality of people's lives as they are actually lived is not reflected. And while the religious right may say that this is a goal to strive for and is all the more reason why such definitions should be enforced, the fact of the matter is that insistence on such rigid definitions does far more damage than good. This is evident when we look at conservative attempts (and almost all attempts are conservative) to reform welfare.

WELFARE VERSUS "WEDFARE"

Along with the defense of marriage and the focus on the traditional family, welfare reform is seen as one of the four cornerstones for the salvation of the social order. The nostalgia for the family of yesteryear has deflected the attention of the public from the socioeconomic foundations of many of the most troubling issues facing the contemporary social order. Instead of looking to the economic policies of late-twentieth-century monopoly capitalism for an explanation of the problems associated with poverty, the political and the religious right attack welfare programs themselves. The attack began in the 1980s and vigorously continued in the 1990s. The political and the religious right routinely point to the growing numbers of families headed by single mothers as proof that government-sponsored welfare programs only encourage morally questionable behavior. Fueled by moral panic and backlash politics, the drive to dismantle welfare is rooted in a family values rhetoric that seeks to save the social order from the destruction it is surely courting if it continues to subsidize the sexual immorality and the illegitimate children that are its legacy. Surely, argues the religious right, the way to restore a fallen social order to God's good graces is not through government support of questionable moral behavior; rather, restoration of the traditional family, touted as the best Department of Health, Education, and Human Welfare, is the much preferred solution.[50]

President Lyndon Johnson's War on Poverty is often faulted for its role in creating a welfare state; critics charge that the social problems the program was meant to address merely worsened, leaving in their wake a flood of crime, illegitimacy, alcohol and drug abuse, and rising levels of welfare dependency. Those on the religious right who champion welfare reform charge that welfare has undermined the work ethic and rewarded illegitimacy, thus guaranteeing its own ongoing base of clients. The most disturbing characteristic of welfare, according to its critics, is its "corrosive effect on family structure," resulting in skyrocketing rates of illegitimacy, which has, in turn, worsened nearly all other social problems.[51]

Originally crafted to address "material poverty," the War on Poverty instead encouraged a poverty perpetuated by behavior. Robert Rector, the Heritage Foundation's senior policy analyst on welfare, maintains that "behavioral poverty" is caused by "a breakdown in the values and conduct that lead to the formation of healthy families, stable personalities, and self-sufficiency." Furthermore, behavioral poverty "incorporates a cluster of severe social pathologies, including eroded work ethic and dependency, lack of educational aspiration and achievement, inability or unwillingness to control one's children, increased single parenthood and illegitimacy, criminal activity, and drug and alcohol abuse." Rector believes that material poverty is relatively rare in this country, but that the rate of behavioral poverty is growing rapidly.[52] Others would disagree:

> Linda Jones of the Episcopal Housing Ministry of Greensboro, North Carolina, said she is a mother of three children, a former homeless person and a welfare recipient. Jones, who is also an African American, told . . . of the indignities of the welfare system, particularly how her self-esteem and personal dignity suffered tremendously as a result of receiving food stamps and other federal subsidies. "I hated myself because I would look at my kids and I knew they deserved better than this," Jones said. "Poverty is bad in America and as far as I am concerned, it is a form of violence."[53]

The religious right charges that the expansion of welfare provided an incentive for people to forgo participation in the workforce and to rely instead on the government to provide for them. This flies in the face of the work ethic that good Christian Americans so proudly profess and wrinkles the neatly pressed social fabric. The emphasis on "workfare" for welfare recipients, while helpful in developing skills that will make people more self-sufficient, in reality falls short of its intention. The fact that more than 50 percent of welfare recipients do not have even a high school diploma makes their prospects of earning a living wage dim. To throw them and their families off welfare, as a columnist from the *New York Times* noted, "while pretending their job prospects are anything but bleak is irresponsible, cruel, and potentially tragic."[54] The necessity of a living wage is not so easy to attain:

> The Associated Press . . . reported on a new study that revealed that most families losing benefits under Virginia's welfare reform law have been unable to find jobs that pay enough to lift them out of poverty. Jay Thomas, a Fauquier County social service manager, sums the study up best: "You know as well as I do, if you're salting fries at $5.60 an hour and you've got three kids, you're not going to make it. The state needs to recognize this."[55]

In the eyes of the religious right, the welfare system deliberately posed a threat to the institution of marriage by making the male figure superfluous; a husband, once considered to be an essential breadwinner, becomes a financial liability under the welfare system. For poverty-line families struggling to provide the basics of food, shelter, and clothing for their families, enduring the financial penalty of having a male breadwinner in the household made no economic sense.

The religious right blames the War on Poverty for contributing to the war against the family and cites the rising rate of so-called illegitimate births, especially among African Americans, to prove the point. This collapse of marriage is blamed directly on the welfare system, which is also credited with destroying the institution of the family in low-income communities.[56] The religious right charges that financial penalties accorded two-parent welfare families prohibit the maintaining of strong family ties. Welfare, then, actively aids and abets illegitimacy. Indeed, the Heritage Foundation cites studies showing that at least 50 percent of the increases in out-of-wedlock births in African American communities during the last few decades are due to the availability of welfare.[57] Illegitimacy, in turn, breeds higher crime rates, increased violence, and moral decay. President Clinton was quoted by the Heritage Foundation as admitting that the "rising wave of crime and violence" washing over the nation is connected to the breakdown of the institution of marriage.[58] Thus, the religious right champions the dissolution of welfare, understanding welfare to be yet another not-so-insidious force that lays waste to the foundational institutions of marriage and family.

How shall we respond—those of us who are feminist or profeminist liberation theologians—to this all-out attack on welfare? Who has what to gain by the not-so-gradual whittling away at welfare? What is at stake here? (Or perhaps we should ask, Who is at the stake?) Will the collapse of welfare shore up the besieged traditional family? How will these changes affect the lived realities of poor people's lives? Why are minority communities so clearly targeted? Why has the pejorative term "illegitimacy" been revived, and for what purposes?

The United States, when measured against eighteen industrial nations, is one of the stingiest when it comes to supplying the basics for its citizenry: it does not cover universal health care, family allowances, or paid parental leave. More children and their single mothers live in poverty in this country than in any other advanced industrial nation. According to Judith Stacey, these embarrassing facts reflect an extremely privatized economy and a culture rife with individualism and racial conflict.[59] The 1996 legislation to cut welfare, replacing it with lifetime limits and "workfare," only exacerbates the problem.

I believe that the current attack on welfare is founded in an ethics of superiority. Grounded in the belief that, while poor people may always be with us, they do not necessarily deserve our help, an ethics of superiority capitalizes on the notion that those who "have" are superior to the "have-nots"; those designated the spiritual heads of their households are superior to those who must submit; those who are white are superior (despite recent rhetoric about reconciliation) to those who are African American, Asian, Hispanic, and Native American; those who are God-fearing, Bible-believing, conservative Christians are superior to all those who do not fit those criteria; those who understand that heterosexuality is the only moral option are superior to all those who identify as lesbian, gay, bisexual, or—heaven help us—heterosexuals who support same-gender relationships; those who are, for the moment, able-bodied are superior to those who live with disabilities. There is no room in an ethics of superiority for those whose life experiences and particularities are different from the norm. According to the ethics of superiority, the norm is, after all, ordained by God. And while Christian sympathy for those unfortunate enough to be outside the norm may be acknowledged, there is no sense of responsibility for their well-being, especially if they refuse to adapt themselves to the accepted guidelines. This ethics of superiority is much in keeping with an ideology of control and is a system of rewards for conformist behavior.

There is much ridicule in these trying political times of Clinton's campaign slogan: "It's the economy, stupid." The religious right fervently disagrees with this sentiment, insisting that the moral decline of the country, not the economy, is at issue. However, I maintain that the economy is precisely what fuels an ethics of superiority, an ideology of control. The globalization of the economy, marked by an uneasy transition from the industrial revolution to the age of technology, has created an underclass of unskilled workers who have been "professionalized" right out of the workforce. As the rich have gotten richer, the working poor have watched their jobs being eliminated and their families being forced to live on an unlivable income. The poor who are not lucky enough to be working have been forced into increasingly violent neighborhoods and onto life-threatening, dangerous streets. Something, somewhere, is terribly amiss.

Guess what? It *is* the economy! Those of us who point out that the gap between the rich and poor is widening in the waning years of late monopoly capitalism are often dismissed as socialist agitators. Yes! The Communist phobia, the red-baiting, is still much with us and keeps those of us who are critics of the economy from being effective in influencing public policy. Feminist theorist Suzanne Pharr notes the pervasiveness of this phenomenon:

> When progressive people point to the growing disparity between the rich and poor, conservatives immediately accuse us of "trying to start a class war." Of course, the answer to this accusation is that it is not progressives who began and perpetuate the ongoing warfare against the poor and middle classes of this country; it is those who have redistributed wealth upward, leaving working people without adequate wages.[60]

Red-baiting and the resultant dismissal of economic critics are part and parcel of what we have come to see in previous pages as part of the ideology of control. If criticism can be dismissed, then control can be maintained. Silencing voices of dissent is classic in the struggle of the "haves" to hold on to their power.

Even though the right has endorsed capitalism as God's chosen economy,[61] in its discussions on poverty and welfare the focus has shifted away from any mention of economic issues toward an emphasis on behavior. This shift of focus is evident in Robert Rector's insistence that material poverty does not really exist in the United States and that behavioral poverty needs to be addressed. The contemporary focus, as in the past when help was provided for the "deserving poor" (read, white, widowed women and their children), is on controlling individual behavior, especially the sexual behavior of African American women.

The rhetoric surrounding this attempt at maintaining control is couched most often in the language of "personal responsibility."[62] By insisting that the cause of poverty is merely behavioral, the religious and the political right succeed in creating a climate in which an ethic of superiority thrives. If poverty is caused by irresponsible/immoral behavior, then those persons who are poor are inferior to those of us who are not poor. We, then, can more effectively distance ourselves from them and, with clearer consciences, dismiss any sense of responsibility to them.

Exactly what has brought us to this point? As was noted earlier, the American Dream grows increasingly out of reach of the majority of citizens (if the Dream can ever be said to have been anything more than a dream, that is). For many, the American Dream has turned into the American Nightmare. More and more families struggle to make their economic ends meet. Many cannot understand that their failure to "succeed" is not their fault, but is symptomatic of something that has gone terribly wrong. As women of all races and all people of color have entered the workplace, the competition for employment has stiffened. Rising levels of economic anxiety result in a cultural mean-spiritedness and the practice of an ethic of superiority. This manifests itself in a racist, sexist, nationalist, and heterosexist scapegoating that shores up the righteous indignation of those who so desperately want to believe they are superior.

Feminist theorist Suzanne Pharr describes specific incidents (of what she maintains is a "racialization of the issues") that effectively divert attention away from the economy. Such incidents perpetuate racism and distance upstanding citizens from those whose behavior must be controlled. The litany of complaints is as follows: immigrants "take our jobs and use our social services"; "children of color and poor children are destroying our schools"; lesbians' and gay men's attempts to attain civil rights "hurt my job chances"; welfare recipients, "people of color are using or abusing our tax monies so we can't balance the budget"; affirmative action should be done away with because "people of color and women are taking jobs away from deserving white men"; the issue of crime is that "we are pouring tax money into public safety, and we are not safe." And on taxes—"my taxes are being used to support services and programs for the undeserving."[63]

Pharr's detailing of examples of this racialization is extremely helpful. Look at the verbs that are used: "take," "use," "destroy," "hurt," "abuse," "deserve." These words are telling indicators that welfare reform is rooted in an ethic of superiority and an ideology of control and is grounded, of course, in fear—or as Marvin Ellison would say, moral panic. Those of the middle class struggling to hang on to what little they have, and those at the top of the economy fighting to keep their power at all costs, believe that those who are poor are grievously at fault. The bottom line communicated is that the increasing numbers of women and children who live in poverty must have done something to deserve it. From the perspective of the religious right, they deserve it because they do not live up to family values. They do not adhere to rigid relational lines as perpetuated by the traditional family of one woman plus one man and children, and they do not conform to strict male-female relational rules of one woman plus one man in lifelong marriage or to the admonition that the man is the head of the family and the woman is to submit. So-called illegitimate children, by their existence, do not conform and therefore are branded for life as "undeserving." Clearly then, because those who are poor do not measure up behaviorally, they are expendable. The following example shows the pain of this position for persons so labeled:

> Jan . . . who describes herself as "a Presbyterian in poverty" . . . told [about] a group of women in her home state of Washington called "the shadow ladies" because they did their grocery shopping at 3:00 A.M. to avoid the judgmental looks and comments of other shoppers when they paid with food stamps. "We had to do it to avoid the pain—it hurts, and the church shouldn't be contributing to it," she said.[64]

This is one example, and a mild one at that, of the insult added to injury in the name of traditional family values. One falls outside the realm of acceptability if one is poor.

Ralph Reed, as was noted in the previous chapter, came up with the solution to poverty: "graduate from high school, get a job and keep it, and get married."[65] While we all know how little jobs pay, presuming one has managed to graduate from high school (for example, $5.60 an hour salting fries at a fast-food restaurant), keeping a job under the current economic conditions is another matter. Those employed at the bottom of the labor market do not, by any stretch of the imagination, make enough to rise above the poverty line. And despite the insistence of the religious right on the panacean properties of the traditional family structure, such families do not provide insurance against poverty. The stability of the traditional family, in many respects, depends upon the level of economic stability that is reached.[66] Enforcing traditional family structures and models of marriage on poor people does nothing to lift them out of poverty and only reinforces an ethic of superiority that maintains control over those whose lifestyles do not conform to the norm.

The emphasis on workfare in contemporary welfare reform has various racist and sexist overtones and is based on the premise that single mothers' dependence on welfare is irresponsible, if not downright immoral and, in conservative Christian circles, un-Christian. We have seen that the religious right would prefer that the woman of the household, especially when she has children, not take on a job in the world of work; the ideal is for her to be at home, taking care of her children and maintaining the home as a haven for her husband. The single-mother welfare recipient is stereotyped as an African American welfare queen, mooching off upstanding taxpayers and thriving economically. The ethic of superiority demands that the "haves" distance themselves as much as possible from the "have-nots." To fail to do so is to admit the humanity of poor people and to begin to think of ways in which they might be just like us. With the stereotype of the African American welfare queen, recipients of welfare are tagged as being undeserving and perpetuating a climate in which the rights of those who "have" are threatened by the "have-nots." Moral panic is in full swing here, and mean-spiritedness thrives.

In the "end of welfare as we know it," the emphasis on motherhood as the fulfillment of female destiny and on women as the keepers of the hearth is not applied. This understanding of female nature does not apply to those not conforming to the appropriate lifestyle. Rather than uplifting the joys of motherhood, the calls of the religious right for welfare reform are punitive and consistently degrade the work of mothering. This contradiction is unique to the subject of welfare:

> The modern welfare state . . . has abandoned the moral mother ideology and diminished the control of mothers over child care. . . . As unpaid caregivers with no connection to a male breadwinner, single mothers are considered undeserving clients of the welfare system. Far from reflecting a liberated view of motherhood, current welfare reform rhetoric casts single motherhood as pathological and advocates policies designed to restore the traditional nuclear family by reinstating the missing male. . . . Part of the reason that maternalist rhetoric can no longer justify public financial support is that the public views this support as benefitting primarily Black mothers.[67]

This racist judgment is a legacy of an ethic of superiority at work. Honoring women who stay home and take care of their children is worthy of praise only if one is white, middle class, and in a heterosexual, lifelong marriage. In short, those who do not measure up to these criteria are inferior and undeserving. It is obviously more acceptable for poor women to be out taking care of other people's homes and children than staying at home to take care of their own. Praised as a worthy female vocation in one circle, it is denounced as irresponsible in another. Illustrative of the deep ambivalence of the religious right's understanding of women and work, middle-class women are accused of "abandoning the needs of their families" in order to pursue fulfillment in the world of work; in poor families, women's lack of work outside the home is caricatured as dysfunctional and debilitating to their children and to society at large.[68] Both circles of women are seen as precipitating a crisis in family values.

In a time of moral panic, political backlash, and economic uncertainty, people of color, women, children, and those whose relationships fall outside the model of traditional marriage are scapegoated. Thus, they are blamed—all too conveniently—for the ills of society. Gone are the appeals to charity or to pity. They are replaced by a cultural and economic system that seeks to do away with those who do not measure up, and in this setting we wonder whether the poor will always be with us. The indicators are that the poor will be abandoned to their fate—a fate, according to some, that they have brought on themselves and thus deserve. At some point, and perhaps much sooner than we expect, the poor will no longer be with us.

RACISM, RECONCILIATION, AND SALVATION

As we have seen with the welfare discourse, racism is alive and well. The agenda to control the "undeserving" poor people on welfare is based on a racist perspective that views African American people as lazy and their children as "predisposed to corruption," the "criminals, crackheads, and welfare mothers" of the future.[69] The welfare debate has focused mainly on white people versus African American people not because white people are without racist sentiments against those of other races; it is mainly indicative of the historical relationships between the two races forged out of slavery, the legacy of which has been racial separation. Thus, white people are labeled as the "haves," and African American people are the "have-nots," who those in power have decided are undeserving.

In keeping with the view that those who are not white are "undeserving" at best, and potential threats to personal safety at worst, Patrick Fagan of the Heritage Foundation wrote in that organization's briefing book for candidates about the disintegration of marriage and the family in contemporary society. In such a context, most especially in poor neighborhoods, the result was the exponential growth of "gangs of young men driven by a destructive credo in place of paternal guidance, young girls vulnerable to abuse, children having children, and mindless, violent crime."[70] He voiced concern about integrating the teenagers of the future into such a society, quoting the dean at a well-known college of criminal justice: "Over the next ten years we will have a 23 percent increase in the number of teenagers in this country. . . . We'll have a 29 percent increase in the number of black teenagers, a 50 percent increase in the number of Latino teenagers. I'm really concerned. I think this is the calm before the storm."[71]

Fagan used this quote to underscore his point that if African American and Latino teenagers could be counted upon to have "solid families with good traditions," there would be no problem. However, since these teenagers are the most likely to have parents who are "economic pariahs" supported by the welfare state, the result is likely to be a weakened social order and nation held hostage by out-of-control, violent recipients of welfare.[72]

This view of Hispanic and African American teenagers is in accord with the subtext of racial anxiety that wends its way throughout the family values discourse.[73] This anxiety breeds a moral panic—in this particular discussion known as illegitimacy and the whole host of social ills accompanying it—and justifies an ideology of control so that those who fit into the traditional models of family can feel safer. Racial anxiety is a prime example of the ethic of superiority. Those in control see the welfare recipient—whom they assume to be African American or Hispanic—as irresponsible, dishonest, morally culpable, unclean, promiscuous, a source of violence, and ultimately, inhuman. In this way those in control—that is, those who are white, nonpoor, and educated—effectively distance themselves from those who are the most economically vulnerable.

Predicated on bridging the distance between the races, Promise Keepers urges those who are active in the group to undertake the process of what is termed "racial reconciliation" by establishing an ongoing connection with a person from a different racial group. The sixth of seven promises made by Promise Keepers reads: "A Promise Keeper is committed to reaching beyond any racial and denominational barriers to demonstrate the power of biblical unity."[74] Unique among the groups of the religious right, Promise Keepers is making an effort at addressing racism, to the shock of some who would probably be content to be surrounded by white faces at conferences. A variety of races is represented on stage, if not in the stands, at Promise Keepers' events. Promise Keepers are encouraged to confess their sins of racism, seek forgiveness, and be reconciled to their brothers of different races. This last step—that of reconciliation—has received the most criticism.

Groups such as the progressive Equal Partners of Faith and the Interfaith Alliance have lodged criticism of this emphasis on reconciliation. They argue that a call for racial reconciliation is not enough in the racist context in which we reside. Reconciliation says nothing about righting the historical wrongs imposed on people of color. To ask for reconciliation before wrongs have been addressed seems to be a bit presumptuous, which is not a good thing to be when you are a white person seeking reconciliation with someone over whom you have power. Just who is being asked to be reconciled and to what? Why should people of color be more reconciled to discrimination, racist violence, and the chipping away of social programs that have benefited their communities?

Equal Partners in Faith[75] also raises concerns about the fact that Promise Keepers fails to speak to its overwhelmingly white membership about white privilege in a racist church and social order. One cannot achieve true racial reconciliation merely by hugging a person of another race—as Promise Keepers are urged to do. In an article in *The Nation*, critics of the Promise Keepers' focus on reconciliation maintain its insufficiency for addressing the sins of racism:

> The warm and fuzzy rhetoric of "reconciliation" conceals some subtexts: The notion that "only changes in people's hearts will make a difference" is a means of avoiding the demand for jobs, community self-determination, freedom from police and criminal violence, and access to housing and educational opportunity. Were the economic program of the conservative backers of this organization—as exemplified by the agenda of the Republican freshmen—ever to be put into practice, the social and economic infrastructure of communities of color would be eliminated. This is fundamental to understanding the essentially regressive racial politics that underlie Promise Keepers' carefully coiffed image.[76]

Preaching racial reconciliation rather than racial justice or racial equality does nothing whatsoever to address the root causes of racism. It effectively controls those with whom one is attempting to right the sins of racism. Not exactly a great start to white repentance, is it? Nowhere in the literature of the Promise Keepers is any mention made of creating social change in order to institute racial equality. No speaker has yet addressed the need for better access of communities of color to jobs, schools, or housing. No mention is made of the rampages of police brutality on men of color or of the criminal violence that ravages communities of color. No mention is made of the high numbers of young people of color who die before they get out of their teens.

Randy Phillips, president of the Promise Keepers, was quoted as saying, in reference to the organization's emphasis on race relations: "The goal is not integration. The goal is reconciling *through* relationships."[77] If this is the case, then we must ask, Exactly to what end is reconciliation urged? In whose interest is it? For what purpose? The problem with emphasizing reconciliation rather than justice is that the social, political, economic, and spiritual consequences of structural racism are kept hidden. Justice demands a shifting of power toward those who have been wronged. Reconciliation allows those in power to maintain control. Justice demands that those with privilege take responsibility for past and present wrongs committed. Reconciliation gets by with a hug. African American social commentator David Love eloquently noted, "If two individuals reconcile, that does not mean they both get what they want. A slave and a slave master may reconcile, but that will not necessarily alter their fundamental relationship."[78] Without a structural analysis of the complexity of racism in this country, no true reconciliation is possible. The reconciliation is premature. Critics of Promise Keepers' focus on reconciliation maintain that the message communicated by Promise Keepers takes the form of "a diversionary political strategy when government programs and policies improving the life for people of color are being defunded and dismantled." The program for racial reconciliation, then, only disempowers and dismisses movements for social justice.[79]

While Promise Keepers tries to project an image of racial inclusivity from its stage, African American speakers who consistently appear at stadium events (such as Wellington Boone, Joseph Garlington, E. V. Hill, and John Perkins) are associated with a branch of the Christian reconstructionist movement (which advocates government according to biblical law) known as Coalition on Revival.[80] This connection with a truly right-wing extremist group does even more harm to efforts to combat racism. Conservative organizations have a history of seeking endorsements from African American and Hispanic communities, choosing to forget the fact that conservative white Christians justified the mass murders of American Indians, upheld slavery, and endorsed Jim Crow laws. Today, the religious right continues to support such efforts as welfare reform, which threatens the ability of poor people to survive. The goal of the religious right has never been to share power with anyone.

Promise Keepers, while being the only ones who so publicly preach reconciliation, are not alone in their theological emphasis on reconciliation. In general, the theology espoused by the religious right would affirm the notion of reconciliation. This notion is popular because reconciled people do not make waves. If people can be reconciled with those who have challenged them, then peace occurs. If those who do not share the political (not to mention, theological) perspectives of the religious right can, nevertheless, be reconciled to those on the religious right, control is made that much easier for the right to maintain. The good thing about reconciliation for those who want to maintain the status quo is that, with reconciliation, no change in business as usual is necessary. People agree to disagree. Injustice goes unaddressed. The boat goes unrocked.

Another facet of the racism of the religious right is the cry that they are the victims of discrimination at the hands of a hostile secular culture. This image of the religious right does not occur readily to those outside the movement. However, as religious scholar Justin Watson maintains, this appeal to victimization is an appeal to be taken seriously. Watson suggests that due consideration be given to this appeal since members of the religious right take their sense of themselves as victims as seriously as they do their nostalgic longing for the days when all was well and America was a Christian nation. Since themes of victimization from the heathen world permeate Christian tradition, Watson maintains that it is natural for the religious right to perceive themselves as being in much the same situation. To dismiss prematurely the extent to which claims of victimization are and will be used in contemporary politics would be to fail to understand the role this dynamic plays in the theology, political strategy, and goals of the religious right.[81] One recent example was the Istook Religious Freedom Amendment voted down in the summer of 1998. This amendment sought to prevent the victimization of Christians in the United States.

Although it would be foolhardy to dismiss the religious right's claim to victimization, the claim is problematic from a variety of viewpoints. The rhetoric of the religious right in relation to claims of victimization is all too often voiced in a manner that compares the right's struggles to those of victims of rape or genocide. As noted in the previous chapter, one of the most glaring examples was in a speech that Pat Robertson gave at William and Mary Law School in which he compared the crime of the gang-rape of a teenage girl to the rape of "our nation's religious heritage, our national morality, of time-honored customs and institutions," committed at the hands of "liberal predators."[82] In a similar fashion, James Dobson has compared the plight of conservative Christians to that of the Jewish people in Nazi Germany.[83]

These comparisons to situations in which people's lives were threatened and/or lost are absolutely unacceptable. In the first place, such comparisons trivialize the devastating scope of genocidal campaigns and sexual violence. Second, the comparisons draw attention to and lend credence to their claims of victimization. Third, the comparisons steal the experiences of one class or group of people. In the genre of feminist liberation theology such actions are called "appropriation." Comparing a gang-rape to the alleged compromise of the nation's religious heritage just does not compute. No one's physical safety was threatened; no one will have nightmares for years; no one will have to pay a huge therapy bill; no one will have flashbacks; no one's ability to trust enough to form intimate relationships has been shaken.

Comparing the contemporary struggles of the religious right to the plight of Jewish people in Nazi Germany is totally inappropriate. Are U.S. Christians forced to live in ghettos? Are their homes and businesses looted and closed down? Are their families forced to flee for their lives? Is anyone in this country starving to death because of being Christian? Is a conspiracy afoot in this land to kill off Christians? Are millions of Christians in this country being murdered because of their faith and cultural heritage? As I sat at the Christian Coalition's 1998 Road to Victory Conference, the woman sitting next to me, in response to a speaker's reference to abortion, commented, "And they said the Holocaust was bad." Such sentiments and comparisons cheapen, trivialize, and do violence to Jewish experience and cultural heritage. They contribute to anti-Semitic tendencies of the theology and practices of the religious right. They perpetuate racism against Jewish people.

This is not to say that those on the religious right cannot feel as if they are under fire and express their frustration over their concerns; that is their privilege as U.S. citizens. It is not acceptable, however, to misappropriate others' experiences of violation and genocide. For a white wealthy man to use images of gang-rape when talking about religious freedom is for him to exercise his power as a white wealthy man. He is not threatened by gang-rape; his physical person will not be injured. His power protects him. Similarly, for Christians to use images of the Holocaust when speaking from their context in the United States is for them to exercise their power as white (primarily) Christian Americans. They are not threatened by imprisonment; they and their families will not be killed for their beliefs. Their power protects them. Those who misappropriate others' experiences employ an ethic of superiority and a theology of ownership. In these two cases, their power—on the one hand, as a white wealthy man, and on the other, as white Christian Americans—allows them to steal someone else's experiences. Because they are not like those who have been violated and murdered, because something like that could never happen to them, they feel entitled in their superiority to use those images to advance their causes. Such misuse assists them in the effort to maintain control of their power.

FROM POWER OVER TO POWER WITH

We are created in God's image, all of us, female and male. This credo is meant to affirm us and bless us, not to constrain us in rigidly defined gender roles in which one gender has more power than the other. Nor is it meant to limit the possibilities of who we can become in this world and how we might best use our gifts. In the same way, marriage and family can be wonderful places in which we are nourished and in which we grow. By the same token, they can also be places of terror in which people are abused and in which they die. The social structures of marriage and family are meant to be examples of relationship. In that frame of reference, then, marriage is not to be seen as the only form of relationship; families are not to be closed to admission of those who are different. Both present possibilities of human relationship; they must not be understood as requirements for human relationships.

Those who want to return this country to the days when the American Dream was alive and well have overlooked the fact that those days were few in number. As we have seen, the American Dream, constructed out of post–World War II relief and hope, was short-lived and really never touched the lives of those who were not white and middle class. Contemporary attacks on welfare underscore the bankruptcy of the American Dream for those who have never fit in. Indeed, the debate over making sure the "undeserving" do not receive unwarranted help makes clear that the American Dream (that is, the benefits accorded to good Christian, Bible-believing, upstanding citizens) is not accessible to all. Furthermore, the suggestion that reconciliation should be sought has neglected a few basic steps, without which reconciliation will be pointless. Reconciliation is used to maintain silence, to smooth over potential ruffles in the social fabric, and to get on with the agenda at hand.

The ideology of control, the ethic of superiority, and the theology of domination have all been used to maintain one vision of human relationships. Faced with challenges to that vision and the possibility of change, those on the religious right have triggered a moral panic and backlash mentality. The power of this movement cannot be dismissed easily, and no matter how nervous it may make us, it should not be ignored. These are the arguments that currently affect our lives, whether or not we are cognizant of that. These are the arguments that could well be legislated into our lives. In the following pages, we will begin to construct another way of viewing these issues. As upstanding people of faith concerned about justice in this society, we must attend to the burning issues of the day before they consume us.

5

Faith, Freedom, and Family

Faith is not meant to be confined to monasteries or to atrophy
behind stained-glass windows. It is supposed to change the way
we live, how we treat each other, how we organize our own
families and, by extension, the national and human family. That
impulse always has a political dimension, and it is the very
essence of an active faith.[1]

Ralph Reed

After spending the last couple of years with this subject material,
I am filled with a longing to move from a place of defense, away
from a place of offense, to a place where those of us who seek
justice-love in our daily lives can begin to formulate creative and
constructive visions of our lives together instead of merely rely-
ing on knee-jerk responses. This chapter draws on some basic feminist liberation theological assumptions, which include our creation as children of God, the ongoing process of liberation (which
others might call salvation) in human history, and the notion of
God-incarnate-with-us. A concept of family inclusive of those
voices excluded by the religious right is spelled out by emphasizing the paradigm of justice rather than judgment. Inclusion, not
exclusion—justice, not premature reconciliation; an ethic of compassion, not an ethic of superiority—is the order of the day.

The previous chapter examined how the focus of the religious
right on gender roles and same-gender relationships is construed
as a theological issue of creation and how the yearning of the religious right for the good old days of yesteryear as manifested in
traditional marriage and family configurations, as well as in the
attempts at welfare reform and racial reconciliation, are the one,
true way to salvation. In this chapter, the focus is on weaving the

theo-ethical themes of creation, liberation, and incarnation together in a way that moves those of us who are progressive, justice-loving people of faith forward into a life-giving, constructive
response to the narrow and life-choking discourse of the religious
right.

CREATION AS CHILDREN OF GOD

> That cause can neither be lost nor stayed
> That takes the course of what God has made;
> And is not trusting in walls and towers,
> But slowly growing from seeds to flowers.[2]

We are all created as children of God; we are all God's children.
That credo is basic to Christian faith. That being the case, how do
we interpret this doctrine of creation in terms of gender issues?
First, let us affirm that difference is a good thing. It makes life
both complicated and interesting. Indeed, it is such a good thing
that it does not have to be controlled. This is really good news for
those of us who had heard about male headship and female submission. It is especially good news for those of us who might have
had to submit to a male someone who had been told he had the
God-given duty to wield power over us. Fortunately, those of us
with feminist, womanist, and *mujerista* sensitivities have failed to
take the message seriously.

MOVING BEYOND TRADITIONAL BOUNDARIES

That cause can neither be lost nor stayed
That takes the course of what God has made . . .

The fact that God created humanity in two genders (some might
even claim more) means that people experience the world differently through their biological gender. People also experience gender in a variety of ways that are socially constructed. But the important point is that all of the energy and worry that has gone
into deciding which gender should do what, when it should be
done, how it should be done, and with whom is unnecessary. The

genders do not have to complement each other. The complementarity theory, used as a means of control, is not necessary or even helpful from a feminist liberation constructive position on creation and gender. Feminists discovered this long ago when we started hearing one another into speech[3] and began sharing our stories with one another. And once the members of the subjugated class start talking with one another, then it is all over. It was bound to happen, sooner or later. We found out that the stories that we had been told to keep us in line were just that—fictional tales designed to keep one group of people holding the power over another group. We suspected as much and then went out and confirmed it.

Realizing that the necessity for male headship and female submission is neither particularly Christian nor at all necessary requires that individuals of both genders engage in getting to know themselves. Once freed from a controlling apparatus of gender dos and don'ts, women and men must decide what part of the way they present themselves as gendered beings in the world is true to their core. A woman may still decide after such soul-searching that she wants to stay home and raise her children. That decision should be as respected as much as any other decision she might have made. The same holds true when a man decides he wants to stay home and raise his children. (Of course, if that particular woman is coparenting with that particular man, sooner or later, they might have to toss a coin.) By getting to know our true selves, we gain the ability to weed out others' perceptions of who we are from the reality of who we are.

This debunking of gender roles and gender complementarity is especially useful for the survival of lesbian women, gay men, and bisexual people, who have been victimized by it. The ideology of control so desperately promulgated by the religious right has been death-dealing to those who do not conform to the heterosexual ideal. The message sent to lesbian, gay, and bisexual people by the religious right—"convert or go away"; "accept the cure for homosexuality or suffer the consequences in a hostile society that will not embrace you as a child of God"[4]—has put conditions on God's unconditional love. Realizing that one is lesbian or gay or bisexual in a hostile cultural setting consumes an enormous amount of energy; knowing that one does not have to be heterosexual in order to be an upstanding child of God enables one to overturn the tyranny of biological destiny and shape one's own life. Only when one understands that one is created in the image of God and is blessed, whether female or male, lesbian, gay, bisexual, or heterosexual, can one then move forward in any decisive way and get on with one's life.

Only when one has debunked the myths of gender complementarity, male headship, female submission, and compulsory heterosexuality can one move beyond the suffocating boundaries of what have been deemed God-ordained rules of gender. The creation of two genders was never meant to construct a narrow, rule-laden road to human fullness and God's grace. God never ordained a certain way for the two genders to interact. The patriarchal order of the world, of power in the hands of one select group of people (male, white, moneyed, heterosexual), was never intended to mark out the one, true, and only route to God. Such jockeying for control has only stayed the cause and dammed up the course of what God has made. For lesbian women, gay men, and bisexual people, accepting their sexuality is much about accepting themselves the way God created them. The issue of creation is theologically central. If we believe that creation happened only once, then we have effectively stopped any possibility of God's continuing to create. Creation is ongoing; we are daily re-created as persons of faith; in fact, we participate with God in the act of creating.[5] God's creative activity with us is unending. And it is good.

Constructing an Inclusive Concept of Family

And is not trusting in walls and towers . . .

When looking to construct an inclusive concept of family, those of us who are pro-feminist and feminist liberation theologians do not trust in building walls and towers. We have seen too much of that, and we are well aware of the damage that can cause. To build walls and towers means to wall ourselves off from other people and look down from our solid towers of superiority. Such has it been with the religious right's insistence that family equals one woman plus one man, united in holy matrimony, with children. The fact that the religious right is so intent on defining people *out* of family has done more damage than anything. It is time to question how much good it does to exclude people from family. Isn't family supposed to be about loving people—unconditionally, I have heard—and welcoming people home? Are we so afraid that the love supply will run out that we wind up hoarding it and applying it to only a select few? Are we so insecure in our families that we feel the need to proclaim our type of family as the only legitimate kind to have, to insist that God blesses only our type of family, to pass laws protecting only our kind of family? Is the next step to outlaw other types of families?

The Family, glorified by the religious right as an exclusive club, is under siege. Apparently, there are people knocking at the door wanting to get in. Those people have names: they are feminists; they are single mothers and their children; they are older citizens living together without "benefit of clergy" so they do not lose their Social Security benefits; they are young, heterosexual couples living together; they are gay men; they are lesbian women; they are conventional families who seek to have an extended family. Their names are legion. The religious right is convinced that they pose a serious threat and, furthermore, that they are to blame for all manner of social ills afflicting our nation and even seek to destroy the social order. Walls are built; towers are raised; love's labor is lost.

A lot of scapegoating is going on here. Convinced of a serious scarcity of love, those who fear letting those "other" people into the family hurriedly build those walls and towers. Perhaps they fear that if they do not protect what they know, there will be no more love for them. Or perhaps they fear a limited amount of salvation is to be had from the God who created us in the first place. And so, by building their walls and towers, they not only seek to defend their views of family and marriage as the one, true way to salvation, but also, ultimately, seek to confine God as well.

And what has this building of walls and towers wrought? It has brought about a climate of fear, shored up an ideology of control, and promulgated an ethic of superiority. Such walls and towers

are difficult to break through. So, what do we do, we who are justice-loving people of faith? Do we keep battering at those walls
and towers? Do we try to argue our way in? Do we try to convince
them that their ways are in vain? This is a serious quandary. Many
of us have family members behind those walls and towers. My
sister has even decorated those walls! Do we stand any chance of
getting them out? Do we stand any chance of reassuring them?

Perhaps these are the wrong questions. Perhaps they are modeled too much on the tactics of the religious right, tactics that we
have found to be quite offensive. I suspect we can get farther by
insisting that we are already part of families, that our families need
no walls and towers, and that our passion for justice-love is blessed
by the One who has created us. Perhaps, when all is said and done,
they will know we are good, strong people of faith by our love.
Surely, we cannot let those who would hide behind defenses of
their own making define us out of our faith, our freedom, or our
families.

That having been said, then, just how do we go about constructing an inclusive concept of family? We begin by doing what we
have already been doing for years. We listen to stories. We all have
them. Who do we say our families are?

Some church school children (ages six to eleven) at Riverside
Church in New York City—a large, interracial, Protestant congregation—were asked to define "family" in a chapel service on
Mother's Day. Since several of the children lived in families without mothers, the staff focused on the more general topic of family. The children responded in ways that revealed their desire to
include absolutely everybody they could. One child said, "A family is two or more people who love each other and live together."
Another child added, "Some family members may not live together, like grandparents, aunts and uncles, or parents who are
divorced." "Family members take care of each other." "Some families have a mommy and a daddy, some only have one parent, some
have two daddies or two mommies, some don't have any parents—just aunts or uncles or grandparents." A seven-year-old girl
noted that they were all part of the church family and that everyone was part of God's family. Pets were included as family members, and the children considered best friends to be like brothers

and sisters, although one boy wished his brother was not part of his family.[6] Revealingly enough, these children had no agenda about excluding people from a family. If anything, they had difficulty defining who was *not* family because they did not want to leave anyone out.

John, a professional white gay man partnered with another professional white gay man in Washington, D.C., defines family as meaning all of the people who live in the same house. He notes, however, that family is much more complex than proximity:

> Even when you explore the complexities of family, Louie and I meet the definition. We are an enduring, stable partnership based on love. We have a wide circle of relatives and friends who share in and benefit from the love our union represents. Our partnership has been acknowledged in a religious ceremony. In some jurisdictions we would be recognized legally. There are some employers who would extend us the same benefits as heterosexual spouses. We are a complementary partnership. Our weaknesses and strengths fit hand-in-glove. We have divided the work and the fun of life between us, easing the burden and enhancing the pleasure. We often are able to face each other without benefit of our public disguises, knowing and accepting the deepest, truest parts of each other. Finally, we know the truth each other means even when we don't have the courage to express that truth. On a practical level, we share the expenses of everyday life. We share a house, a car, and bills. We live our lives as a couple. We are "Louie-and-John" to the people we meet, not just Louie and John. The word family can have no less meaning for us than it does for anyone who might use the phrase "family values" to disenfranchise us.[7]

John's understanding of family is an eloquent description of his partnership/marriage with Louie—a relationship fully grounded in love, respect, and mutuality. Theirs, as John described it, is truly a complementary relationship and thus represents a thorough re-imagining of the gender "complementarity" theory discussed elsewhere. If two men can consider their intimate relationship to be a complementary partnership, what does that do to the authority of gender complementarity employed so often to maintain control over sexuality, women, and all who might pose a threat to the status quo?

Angela, a native of Germany now living in New England, notes the several kinds of family that are part of her life. She refers to her biological family, but the family she has created with her life-partner and other soul mates nourish her in a much healthier way than her biological family was ever able to. This family she has created provides her with a sense of belonging, a circle in which she can count on someone to be there for her and vice versa. This family is a community of responsibility. Angela also describes her "family by adoption," which consists of older friends who treat her as their daughter and have provided parenting when she needed it. To her, they are an idealized wish-they-were-blood family. She sums up her experience of family by observing that family means "a web of formative relationships to which [she] can always return and for whose health and well-being [she] is co-responsible."[8] For Angela, her family is a network of connections, many of which she has created herself. She, too, saw the need to reach out beyond the walls of her biological family, intuitively knowing that there must be family beyond the "traditional" structure.

Jason, a white, thirty-something man in the United States, is searching again for ways to make family. His marriage of ten years broke up. Issues surrounding his sexual identity became too much for his wife to bear. Now with deep grief and some promise of freedom, he balances old and new worlds, reaching out to another man for love without apology while attempting to maintain connections with his young daughter. He wrote,

> One family, the dream of father/mother/child, dies to be reborn in some new shape; my nuclear family gives support while also adding killing swipes of nasty blades; the extended family of in-laws remains limited in its knowledge of my story and a safety net; a beach house holds a lover's family, his non-biological community of support, and all the angst of first introductions. Which family is considered real, which one is valued? It matters little since they all are mine.[9]

Jason's mapping of his constellations of family is notable for his ability to let them shift, be reborn, and form in new shapes. In the midst of chaos comes connection. In the midst of pain comes comfort for him. His understanding of family has not come pre-packaged, guarded by walls and towers. It is in a process of becoming.

Alison, a white Australian woman in her seventies and Episcopal priest who is now living in Maine, notes that her concept of family seems to be getting broader and broader. She writes,

> I think about the interconnectedness of everyone and everything and the phrase "the human family." I don't much like the phrase "the family of God" because it seems to imply that some are excluded. My nuclear family (kids, grandchildren, great grandchildren and their mothers who have come to the family through marriage) are clearly family.... The two divorced wives of my two older sons still feel to me like family. Then there is my Greenfire Community[10] family of about twelve women to whom I am very closely connected. Then there are friends ... [who] ... evoke from me the same response as family does. I would put myself on the line for them.[11]

Alison's understanding of family is an interwoven, interconnectedness, layered upon several generations. Her community and close friends are much a part of that family. The basic point of her understanding of family is, For whom would you put yourself on the line?

Reed, a white man in his early thirties married to a white woman, finds the "traditional" family of a mother, father, and children too limiting as the sole definition of family. He argues that any group of people who love one another can be a family. He notes that as someone who works on Capitol Hill, in the aftermath of the murder of two Capitol police officers in the summer of 1998, there was a feeling of family, even though it was a family drawn together in tragedy. He considers his small church community to be family as well. In terms of more immediate meanings of family, he would describe "family" as including people who live together, have some financial connection, take care of each other, love each other.[12]

Bev, a white woman in her late forties, writes,

> I was blessed to be born into a loving family, with parents who were married until death claimed one of them. Family to me is the easy comfort of being yourself and feeling completely secure. The members of my family love each other and would continue to love each other no matter what. When I go home to visit, I always feel so secure in simply being. I don't have to make conversation if I don't feel like talking. None of us tries to think of things to entertain each other. . . . I think the intolerance of so many who preach family values is what disturbs me the most. . . . We wanted our parents to be proud of us because we thought so much of them, not because we had to be perfect—or else. They were our guidance counselors, and also our dear friends whom we knew loved us for who each one of us was.[13]

Bev, unlike so many, had a wonderful experience growing up in her biological family. She speaks of a certain ease that comes with familiarity, a comfortableness that makes home truly home. She was taught love and tolerance in ways that were not based on hoarding love—for surely, there was more than enough to go around. Her family, while consisting of what most would consider the "traditional" family, is an example of a true sense of coming home, a place in which each child was made to feel loved and so learned to love and love well.

Michele, a white professional, heterosexual woman in her mid-thirties, reminds us that what makes a family is not the bond of blood, but the joy and respect we have in one another's lives. Having seen firsthand the damage that can be done in the name of blood relationship, she has created her own family constellation, always upholding joy and respect as her family values.[14]

Meg, a young white woman of eighteen, whose gay, New York City–based father and Michigan-based mother have coparented her and her two sisters, wrote, "My family has always been a huge support system for me. When I'm doubting myself, they believe in me. Without fail, they see my good qualities; they think I'm funny, smart, beautiful, and the cool thing is that they make me believe it too."[15] For Meg, family is about being there and loving one another.

Judi was eleven years old when she became an only child after the death of her twin sister, Joy. Born and bred in the white, pre–civil rights South, she and Terry, also an only child, had been best friends since the age of eight. During high school and college days, she and Terry dated some. Neither one of them could figure out why kissing did not "work" for them. Now, both in their early fifties, they consider themselves to be sister and brother. Terry lives with his partner of eighteen years, Jon; Judi lives with her partner, Anne. Judi and Terry created a family connection out of no family. They have been family to each other for more than forty years.[16]

Hyun Kyung, a Korean woman teaching theology in New York City, longed for family. Feeling slightly like an outcast in the Korean community, she decided to create her own and "adopted" a brother and a sister who were similarly outcast. Her "brother" is a Korean gay man she befriended. Her "sister" is a Korean woman, married to an African American man. Together, they celebrate birthdays and other special days. They have even bought a home together for when they are in Korea. They have made one another family.[17]

Joan, a white lesbian woman in her early fifties living in New York City, understands family in two distinct ways. The first is the biological birth family, which may or may not include an anonymous parent (either through egg or sperm donors or through rape). The second is the family of choice, a category that changes over time, and the core of which is often known only retrospectively. Family of choice includes people who are not related by blood and is ultimately defined by a commitment to support, love, and be present to one another.[18]

For Kathryn, who is a womanist social ethicist and an African American woman married to an African American man, family has meant obligations. Although this has been burdensome and, at times, unhealthy for her, it has strengthened her moral convictions about the necessity to care for others. She writes,

A major portion of my financial and emotional resources has been directed toward my "family" during my life because I felt it was my duty. . . . I feel that it is good for me to have this "service" dimension as part of my life. I also feel that based on issues related to race and class (I am one of few who have gone to college and beyond in the extended family), I "owe" my family the gift of resources that I have and they don't.[19]

For Kathryn, family has nurtured in her the understanding that you care for your family. She learned that commitment and service were part of what family life entailed. This is a critical point to keep in mind when going about the task of constructing an inclusive concept of family. Family is not always about what the best, most convenient scenario may be for us. It often requires sacrifice, burdens, and carrying out obligations. Family requires chipping in financially to help a cousin, an aunt, a nephew, a sister. It requires building the self-esteem of an eleven-year-old nephew by getting him up in the middle of the night so he will not wet the bed. It requires helping a mother with Alzheimer's disease with her daily hygiene. It requires trips home on vacation time or days off to keep older parents company. It requires forgoing that new sweater you wanted so that your kid can have a new soccer ball. It requires dropping everything and spending time with a suicidal friend. An inclusive concept of family must incorporate an ethic of care—for better or for worse, in sickness and in health. Part of the definition of "family," after all, is about being there, no matter what.

Pam, a white, divorced, professional woman, mother of two boys, who is in a committed relationship with a white man, understands family as "a group of people who share a history, some form of common identity, a commitment to nurture, support, and care for each other over a period of time, all rooted in bonds of affection and emotional intimacy." There is usually an intergenerational character to family, with interconnections to both preceding and succeeding generations. She is disturbed by the extent to which the religious right wants to "force one definition of family on all the rest of us as somehow natural, rather than accepting the diversity of families and adopting policies that help [all] families [to] flourish."[20]

Jann, a white woman living in New York City who is in a partnered relationship with a Hispanic woman, says that her definition of family requires community. She writes, after a conversation with a friend who had commented that families are not what they used to be, "It struck me that it is not the family that is in demise, it is community that is in demise. Transiency due to economic realities has virtually eliminated stable communities." She adds, "Family is not just who I live with; it includes the layers of people who are committed to supporting me and my most intimate family."[21]

This especially critical point is too many times forgotten. In those good old days of yesteryear, many of us had community within our neighborhoods. Neighbors were always watching out for one another's children; teachers knew the families of the children they taught; doctors knew you as a person and not as a file number. Those were the days when your parents knew you had misbehaved from the neighborhood grapevine—before you even walked in the door. Those were the days when you were known as "Floyd Bathurst's granddaughter" or "Dick Gilson's daughter" or "Claudia's sister."

The toll wreaked by economic instability has eroded that sort of neighborhood. People move frequently for jobs, work more hours, and generally live at a much faster pace. Those who struggle to survive in this economic system often find themselves moving from place to place in order to find affordable accommodations. Many find themselves living in neighborhoods plagued by violence. Many are afraid to let their children play outside. Many are afraid to trust their neighbors.

So, yes, family does require community in order to thrive. Community as a locus and resource for our families is critical. It is a part of the infrastructure, if you will, of our families. This is not a new insight. But it is important that it be in our consciousness: our families should not be any more isolated than they already are. This support is critical for all families; it is especially critical for families that do not fit the definition of the "traditional" family.

These stories are just a few of the many stories waiting to be told. Very few of these families would be accepted as "true" families in the eyes of the religious right. Those whose families might meet the traditional definition would not want to be included in the "family canon" of the religious right. These families have never trusted in walls and towers; indeed, they have never seen the need in the first place for building walls and towers. What might we glean from these stories to help us in the building of an inclusive concept of family?

FAMILY AS RESOURCE

But slowly growing from seeds to flowers . . .

The new family diversity, to which so many of us can testify, is rich indeed. What does it teach us about models of family life? What does it teach us in terms of using the new family diversity to address contemporary crises? All of these stories have involved questioning what has appeared to be unquestionable. Fueled by a sense that there had to be other models possible beyond the walls and towers, many found themselves creating new models of family that were more inclusive. These new models, this new family diversity, more adequately met the everyday needs of people and more accurately reflected the lived realities of their lives. Where their biological families could not meet their needs, they created other family constellations.

Often turning traditional norms of family life around, those who reflected on the nature of family creatively broke away from structures that would narrowly channel familial love. John, writing about his complementary relationship with Louie, unknowingly offers a new take on the theory of gender complementarity. He offers us a resource for finding complementarity within a relationship between two people rather than from an outwardly imposed criterion. Complementarity within a relationship gives us something to work toward; it assumes that relationships are growing, in need of nurture, and that, given attention, they will flower into relationships of mutuality.

Angela knew that other resources had to be out there beyond the traditional family structure. Over the years, she built up a family that provided a sense of belonging. Her family constellation turned into a community of responsibility. This community of responsibility is not one that seeks to constrain its members; rather, it branches out into wider circles. This is a marvelous model for addressing crises facing today's family. Based on inclusivity rather than a defensive exclusivity, family as a community of responsibility can move beyond its temporal and local context to provide a resource for wider, and overlapping, circles of community. A community of responsibility also puts us on notice that there are people who care about what is happening in our lives, who hold us accountable, and who stand ready to challenge us. Family is not always about providing a safe haven away from the headaches of the world. Family needs to be a place that will love you enough to challenge you. Family members want to know the details. Our lives affect theirs. Their lives affect ours. In short, our communities of responsibility are affected by other communities of responsibility. With this understanding of family and community, we are no longer isolated. We stand ready to branch out and grow beyond where we have been planted. And, as Alison noted, we stand ready to put ourselves on the line for one another.

We must be open to change during these challenging times for families and the wider social order. Out of the chaos of change comes connection. Out of confusion over changing roles come self-knowledge and clarity. As in Jason's changing family situation, we must be open to the fact that to remain viable, families, like the wider community in which they are rooted, shift shape. That should not threaten us; instead, it should provide hope for us to know that our creation as children of God is ongoing and that we have a role as cocreators with God. Creation is never finished, once and for all. Being alive, being people of faith, means that we are continually being re-created and are re-creating.

Reed's reference to families and communities being drawn together in times of tragedy is important. It bursts the bubble of the always happy family in those golden days of yesteryear. Tragedy brings people together. It strengthens us and our ties to one another. It reminds us of our love for one another. It keeps us from being too complacent or too comfortable. It can spur us on to act for justice. And as Kathryn so clearly pointed out, when trouble happens, part of being a member of a family or of a community is being there for one another, picking up the burden when others can no longer carry it, sharing our wealth when others need help surviving, sharing our power so that we and they are not alone.

The Riverside Church School children may have taught us the best lesson of all: they were unable to say who was *not* family. They did not want to hurt anyone's feelings; they felt compassion toward anyone who might feel left out. The children naturally included their pets in family, recognizing immediately the companion role that animals play in our lives. Building walls and towers to keep others out would have been the last thing they were capable of doing. These children wanted to scatter seeds and watch the miracle of growth. As some of the adults surveyed in this chapter showed, we do not always lose our childhood inclinations to be inclusive—though often, as adults, we have to find our way back to it through a circuitous and sometimes painful route. What Joan describes as a family of choice, Michele describes as a familial bond of joy and respect, and Bev talks about as a place where you can be yourself reflects choices that, as adults, we have been empowered to make. Being able to include others in our original circle of family or choosing not to include biological family members who may have caused us physical or psychological harm is critical to a model of family in which growth is possible and welcomed. Hyun Kyung, with her family of outcasts, and Judi, with her adopted brother, show us how to make a family out of no family. If we were behind walls that would defend a narrow definition of who could be family, this would not be possible. We would not be able to free ourselves from abusive and controlling biological family members, and we would not be able to include those who mattered most to us and lived somewhere beyond that wall. Making a family out of no family, opening our arms to make sure that those we love are not left out (and also that those loved by others are able to be included in their families), is critical to growing strong families and strong communities.

TOWARD LIBERATION

> Each noble service that we have wrought
> Was first conceived as a fruitful thought;
> Each worthy cause of a future glorious
> By quietly growing becomes victorious.[22]

We cannot stop with the construction of an inclusive concept of family. That task is ongoing and, by design, unfinished, yet it will ultimately fail if not combined with efforts to seek justice on behalf of others as well as ourselves. Creation is only part of the picture; as we know, it is only the beginning of the story. The movement toward liberation, the movement toward what the religious right calls salvation, must be part of a constructive response. Without what would call us to justice, we, too, would eventually build walls and towers.

Beyond Liberalism

Each noble service that we have wrought was first conceived as a fruitful thought . . .

The difference between those who advocate liberalism and those who seek justice is that when the backlash begins, liberals retreat. They urge caution and speak of the high cost of supporting those whose lives run counter to the pattern proscribed by the religious right. Those who seek justice, though they may be just as worried about backlash fallout, know that there is no going back and that there can be no toning down of demands for justice. They know the price to pay is high; they know, too, that the closer they get to justice, the worse the backlash will be.

Feminist liberation theologian Carter Heyward urges church people and activists for social change to hang on to their commitments to justice. This, she maintains, is absolutely essential in a world-church that is so divided:

> It is important that those of us in the christian church be clear that our strong emphasis on justice—sexual and gender and ra-

166 A FEMINIST RESPONSE

cial and economic justice—is rooted in a commitment to struggle for right relation, not to divide and separate women from men, gay from straight, white from other colors, or middle class from poorer or richer people. The fact is, our christian body, and the body of creation itself, is fragmented, splintered, terribly, horribly divided. This is our context, the actual situation in which our vocation is to help find, and help lead, the way toward the healing and liberation of our body, as christians, as humans, and as God's creatures who share the earth. We cannot help lead unless we are able and willing to see and hear and speak truth as best we can, including the horrendous truths of the violence and injustices that threaten to undo us all.[23]

Heyward's insistence on countering the divisiveness that threatens the well-being of all of us is critical in the movement beyond liberalism. While many liberals want unity in the church or in the social order almost more than anything and thus would do almost anything to avoid divisiveness, this is not what Heyward intends. Such avoidance of controversy only shores up injustice; it gives in to the demands of the religious right. Silence only protects the interests of those who want to maintain the unjust status quo. Speaking the truth, especially when it would be easier to retreat in the face of backlash, is absolutely critical to the movement toward justice. Without truth-speaking, justice will not prevail.

One of the problems with the liberal approach to injustice is that people seem to have no deep-seated passion for real change. Without such passion—or what Heyward would call "our passion for justice"[24]—only surface issues get attention. The roots of the matter and the wider implications are never really examined in full. A liberal approach is always concerned with the broader institutional politics and is not a systemic approach.

Those who are concerned with delivering justice find themselves, from time to time, realizing just how interconnected we all are. What might begin as an effort to pay women the same as men leads to a discussion of the social construction of gender roles, which, in turn, leads to a discussion of male headship, which then leads to an examination of traditional marriage. And on it goes.

The ways in which the issues in this book are interconnected are many; in fact, the issues that we have explored in these pages are connected much more widely to issues we have not even been able to discuss. But hear this point: justice is a web of interconnected movements, events, and people! The work of liberation is ongoing. And it is inherently a *relational* movement.[25]

As we engage in the work of liberation, in our movement toward justice, we are making connections among and between us; we are reconnecting things that have been separated. When we raise issues about the outcome of welfare reform, for instance, we must make many connections: the issues of racism, sexism, classism, and xenophobia are several that come to mind immediately. This is not meant to be overwhelming; to the contrary, such interconnections between issues, between people, signify something important in the movement toward liberation. We are not alone! Our "noble service," as intoned in the hymn, should never be construed as taking place in isolation. Rather, the "fruit" of collective, gathered community effort matters.

RECONCILIATION WITH JUSTICE

Each worthy cause of a future glorious by quietly growing becomes victorious . . .

Many of us who work for justice have heard from liberal church leaders of the importance of reconciliation. This has typically been the case when discussing issues of race and of sexuality. The church leaders, caught as they are in the politics of their positions, speak earnestly about hearing the pain of both sides. They then urge both sides to be reconciled with each other. The problem with this approach is that several key steps have been left out. First of all, listening to the pain of both sides requires analysis. The pain of those who have been discriminating against others, who feel that their rights are being infringed upon because they do not believe in racial justice, the ordination of lesbian/gay people, or the ordination of women (pick your topic), must be viewed as the pain of people who desperately want to maintain the status quo and hang on to their power. Their pain is the pain of the oppressor.

The pain of those who have been discriminated against is radically different. Theirs is the pain of the oppressed, the pain of those who are tired of being invisible, silent, and subjugated. Theirs is the pain of people going up against societal and ecclesiastical structures time and time again to seek justice. Theirs is the pain of people being denied yet again. Theirs is the pain of people who do not have any say in matters affecting them.

For church and political leaders to urge reconciliation at this point only exacerbates the injustices being perpetrated against women, people of color, and lesbian women and gay men. Of course, liberal leaders are not the only ones at fault here. As we have seen, Promise Keepers urges racial reconciliation and suggests at its stadium events that white men turn to men of color near them and hug them as a sign of their desire to be reconciled. Now, how in the world is a hug going to address the historical wrongs imposed on people of color? And given that so many groups on the religious right do all they can do to shape public viewpoints and policy on matters that devastate communities of poor people and people of color (such as welfare reform), how can people of color be expected to accept this token of reconciliation? This sort of reconciliation is a reconciliation without justice; it is, thus, an enforced reconciliation.

Enforced reconciliation, whether in the context of the liberal church or in the context of Promise Keepers' stadium rallies, perpetuates injustice. It does nothing to serve the cause of liberation. It does nothing to address the concerns of oppressed people. It manages only to soothe the frayed nerves of liberal church leaders who are afraid that political dissension will create further hardships for them. In the context of Promise Keepers and other groups of the religious right, reconciliation only salves the consciences of those who want an easy forgiveness so that people in the United States can "be white without feeling guilty" and "prosper without feeling blamed."[26] In neither case is structural sin examined as a prelude to reconciliation.

Those seeking true reconciliation with justice with those they have harmed must first realize that such reconciliation is a long process. The hemorrhage of prejudice and the resulting flow of devalued personhood cannot be stanched by a simple Band-Aid.

Womanist theologian Delores Williams, writing about the treatment of Black women, notes the following,

> Society's way of devaluing Black womanhood is sin. For Black women's womanhood is their humanity. To devalue Black women's womanhood is to take away their humanity. . . . To devalue any of this understanding of a womanist is to devalue Black women's womanhood, to devalue their humanity, to be guilty of sin—the sin that denies that Black women's humanity is in the image of God as is all humanity.[27]

Perpetrators of racism, sexism, heterosexism, and homophobia—all have devalued the personhood of many. The first step in moving toward reconciliation with justice is to acknowledge historical, structural, and personal sin. Doing this requires doing one's homework. Do not ever ask the one you have been discriminating against to help you process this. That is the oppressor's responsibility. Only after behavior has changed, oppression has ceased, the personhood of the oppressed is valued, and the oppressed have agreed can reconciliation ever proceed.[28]

In the process of moving beyond liberalism toward justice, we must remember that making connections, reconnecting what has been systematically disconnected, is crucial to sustaining the journey. If we let fear rule our lives, then we will turn our backs on justice, retreat from the line just when we are most needed, and cash in our liberal privilege when the struggle becomes too inconvenient. The knowledge that there are many interconnections to be made in the structural web of oppression has the potential to create a strong justice-centered movement. Connecting, reconnecting, and interconnecting shore us all up and provide momentum for our movement.

INCARNATION—GOD-WITH-US

> Thereby itself like a tree it shows;
> That high it reaches as deep it grows;
> And when the storms are its branches shaking,
> It deeper root in the soil is taking.[29]

The storms created by the insistence of the groups of the religious right that their way of marriage and family life is the one and only true way to salvation have resulted in a great deal of injustice against all those whose lives differ from theirs. Single parents; lesbian, gay, and bisexual people; persons living together; and welfare mothers (and their so-called illegitimate children) have borne the brunt of discrimination. The storm does not show signs of subsiding anytime soon. To weather the storm, we must make sure that our roots are placed deep in community and that our branches have extended to other sisters and brothers in the struggle.

Carter Heyward has noted that "the God whom Jesus loved was, and is, no master of control."[30] This observation is, I believe, key to an incarnational approach to struggles for justice. The ethic of superiority, the theology of domination, the ideology of control—all presuppose a God who is a Master of Control. Pat Robertson frequently admonishes that if America does not collectively repent and turn from its wicked ways, God will seek vengeance. The gay-friendly city of Orlando, Florida, will be hit with hurricanes and meteors, and the hedge of protection hitherto placed around the nation will no longer be guaranteed. Much of the religious right's theology is formulated on the assumption that God is a punishing God, who has prescribed a narrow way of carrying on human relationships. If homosexuals do not repent and seek to be cured, they will be lost forever. If welfare mothers do not welcome men into their lives, their children will be forever outcast, and they will always be poor. If people of color do not accept the religious right's overtures of reconciliation, people of color themselves will be held responsible for racism. If women do not graciously submit to their husbands, they will be held responsible for the downfall of civilization.

God is very much a Master of Control in this scenario. That control, after all, holds the family, the social order, and the entire nation together. This Master of Control holds sway over life and death. Men model themselves in the image of Him. And women understand that they are to submit to Him, for if they graciously submit, then the Master of Control is a benevolent Master. If one mollifies this Master of Control, then one stands a chance of succeeding. But the problem here is that the Master of Control posits an atmosphere of alienation, disconnection, and cutthroat competition. Feminist theorist Suzanne Pharr points to some of the effects of this atmosphere:

> We are seeing a rapid rise of mean-spiritedness, fed by talk radio and television, the rhetoric of cynical politicians, and the embittered disillusionment of people whose hopes and dreams have been destroyed and whose lives feel threatened. It is a mean-spiritedness that seems to feed upon itself, seeking everywhere someone to blame, someone who is the cause of this pain, this disappointment, this failure to succeed. The airwaves are filled with rancor and anger, cynicism and accusation. Recently, I have been asking people to describe the mood of the country. They respond, "depressed, angry, overwhelmed, feeling isolated and cut off, mistrustful, mean, hurt, fearful."[31]

This environment emerges when people feel that they have played by the rules, obeyed the Master of Control, and done all the "right" things. After all, a Master of Control promises rewards to those who have played by the rules. Success comes to those who have kept to the straight and narrow path. In the waning days of late-twentieth-century monopoly capitalism, success is no longer to be had. With increased domestic and international turmoil in the economy, life is plagued with uncertainty. Layoffs loom on the horizon; savings accounts are depleted; new jobs are difficult to find. Those who have been promised the American Dream have looked around and failed to spot it. Mean-spiritedness rules the day. Those who seek justice on behalf of lesbian, gay, and bisexual people, poor people, and people of color are met by an attitude laced with anger and a gnawing despair that soon nothing will be left for those who have always lived by the rules. Moral panic ensues, and fear rules the day.

A feminist liberation theo-ethical perspective must insist, as Heyward has done, that God is no Master of Control. With this assumption grounding our work, those of us who are pro-feminist and feminist liberation theologians can begin to reshape an incarnational theology of God-with-us. This incarnational theology is about empowering ourselves and others and sharing our power with those who need it most. An incarnational theology of God-with-us is rooted in the deep soil of community; it is also invested in branching out to reach those who themselves struggle for justice. Accountability to others is key, and a solidarity that pushes beyond the comfortable liberal positions is essential.

Mujerista theologian Ada María Isasi-Díaz argues for a solidarity that is deeper than the popular meaning of "being in agreement with." This sort of solidarity is a comfortable, unchallenging position, possessed of little depth. Isasi-Díaz writes that solidarity has to do with "understanding the interconnections that exist between oppression and privilege, between the rich and the poor, the oppressed and the oppressors. It also refers to the cohesiveness that needs to exist among communities of struggle."[32] Solidarity is not easy, and it should never be considered as such. It requires ongoing work, a community of accountability, the willingness to be challenged on issues, and an openness to change.

Solidarity is absolutely critical to an incarnational theology. God-with-us is about being in relation, being in community, pushing to reach new horizons, and striving forward in pursuit of justice. It is never about being comfortable; it is always about struggling to work through conflicts. Solidarity cannot afford to be about offering safe space, except to those who are in danger. If safe space is taken to mean a space free from being challenged, then that is not conducive to the work of solidarity. Such requests for safe space impede justice work; appeals to safe space cloak a desire to remain untouched and untouching. Solidarity must remain strongly rooted in the soil of community to withstand storms while freely branching out to connect to others.

Creating, Liberating, and Incarnating in the Struggle

Today, in the here and now, we live in a great deal of tension. The national climate—as we saw recently in the attempt of a Republican Congress, dominated by the concerns of the religious right, to bring down a Democratic, sort of liberal, president—is one of chilling mean-spiritedness. Even though this attempt was not successful, the extent to which members of the religious right establishment were willing to sidetrack government business in the name of so-called family values was truly astonishing. We live in a time characterized by political, physical, and spiritual violence against those who are different. Unlike the religious right that claims to be victimized, we know that for far too long we have been victims. We know this because we have literally counted the bodies. In October of 1998, we added one more: that of a young college kid, Matthew Shepard, viciously murdered by kids from the local community, allegedly (we have to say allegedly) because he was gay. The rage with which his "differentness" was met should remind us all that backlash politics and the ethic of superiority that shores it up are alive and well. His murder was publicized; many of the murders among us are not.

We cannot deny that we have been, and are, victims. The ravages of racism, sexism, heterosexism, and anti-Semitism have, over the years, exacted their toll. But we have not let this fact crush our spirits. So we are, have been, and probably will be victims. We have come too far to let that stop our quest for a justice-love that knows no bounds. Now is not the time to run back to our closets for safety's sake. As many of us know, that safety does not really exist. Now is *not* the time to keep silence. Audre Lorde forcefully reminded us: "Your silence will not protect you."[33] Now is *not* the time to give in to a reconciliation based on the desire to keep the boat from rocking. Rocking boats bring home the point that the time has come to change the course away from a hate-based fear and toward an openness based on justice-love.

We who are justice-loving people of faith must remember that we are created and we create, in all of our differentness, in the image of God, and it is good. We participate in the ongoing struggle for liberation of ourselves and others, and we are blessed. God is incarnate-here-and-now-with-us, and we participate in ongoing incarnation. We are fed. The ongoing action of creating, liberating, and incarnating means that we can never give in to the insistence by the religious right that the relationships among us that "deviate from the norm" of traditional marriage are sick or sinful. We are blessed, and we know it. No fear-based rhetoric, no matter how vitriolic, no matter how effective on a national policy level, can change that. Our families are blessed. We know that the restoration of the so-called traditional family will not save the soul of the nation. We do know, however, that our diverse family configurations are critical to our nurture and survival as a justice-loving people. We know that denunciation of such different kinds of families is not only shortsighted on the part of the religious right, but also betrays a pathetic insecurity that would be pitied if only it were not so dangerous. We must never forget the struggles we have gone through to find and nurture our family networks. Remember the instinct of the children: they wanted to include everybody. We must take that instinct to heart. We are blessed, and we bless. It is good indeed.

Conclusion
Reclaiming Our Lives from the Religious Right

Be then no more by a storm dismayed,
For by it the full-grown seeds are laid;
And though the tree by its might it shatters,
What then, if thousands of seeds it scatters![1]

My sister and I are chronically unable to have a conversation that covers anything of significance. There is a wide gulf between us. I believe she feels threatened by who I am in the world; I am frustrated by my inability to share my life with her. Worse yet, I rarely am able to see her children. One of my sister's heroes is Oliver North; she buys her children videos from Focus on the Family; she believes Jesus was a Christian. She is invested in appearing to have the perfect family. What the true situation is, I really do not know. Despite surface pretenses, we are alienated from each other. Her walls are high; there are no windows.

While some may postulate that there can be no true reconciliation with the religious right, that there can be no changing of adherents' minds, that there can be no true conversations because the starting assumptions are not the same, that is way too pessimistic a point of view for me to hang on to for very long. I began this book with the hope that somehow I could reach in, I could connect, I could even change people's minds. I wanted to save my sister. The irony is, of course, she undoubtedly wants to save me. But here is where the great disconnect is: we mean entirely two different things by the word "save." She wants to save me from what she views as a destructive lifestyle, one not in keeping with the traditional values of God, country, and family. I want to save her from a narrow existence, shored up by walls and towers; I want to save her from a fear-based mentality that underscores the belief that God declared only one way to be in intimate relation with another and only one way to be family. I want to save her so that we can be sisters in the true sense of the word. I want her blessing on my life. Heck, I want her back in my life.

I am sure that this quandary affects many of us. The religious right is not just an impersonal political movement that threatens our values of justice-love; it consists of those we know. I believe, somewhere deep in my heart, that at some time, somehow, and with the grace of God, some point of connection will come between these two disparate communities—the religious right and those of us who seek justice. This is not to say that either side will ever agree with the other. But what I hope will happen is that we will be able to connect, to see the other's humanity, and perhaps someday find a way to respect the other. The problem is that day is undoubtedly long in coming. It requires that one group not try to legislate away the other's rights. It requires that one group refrain from damning the other to hell. It requires standing up for justice.

In the meantime, it requires living in the "in between" time, the time of not yet, the time of waiting. This "in between" time is characterized by three stages of action: be unrepentant, be of good faith, and cultivate holy impatience.

BE UNREPENTANT

I am the unrepentant. It has always been so. Indeed, it has been the cause of a great deal of head shaking on my parents' part over the years. They call it the "Gilson stubbornness." I think I got it from my paternal grandfather; my father has it too. Wherever it came from, it always stands me in good stead in the struggle for justice. The religious right calls us to repentance.

- Those of us who are on welfare are called to work and to wed. We are promised legitimacy for our children in return. No one, however, has promised us a living wage.
- Those of us who are African American, Asian, Hispanic, and American Indian are called to a premature reconciliation. We are promised a hug in return. No one, however, has promised us any relief from the toll exacted by racist violence.

- Those of us who are uppity women are called to submission. We are promised a man who will lead us spiritually in return. No one has asked us *whether* we want to be led; no one has asked us *where* we want to be led. No one has bothered to remind us that we are human beings created in God's image and therefore have our own moral agency.
- Those of us who are lesbian women, gay men, or bisexual people are called to convert to a heterosexual identity. We are promised eternal salvation in return. No one has told us that by accepting such a call, we will forever feel incomplete because we will have sold our souls . . .
- Those of us who embrace new configurations of family are called to come to our senses and pay obeisance to the traditional model of family. We are promised the satisfaction of knowing that we have saved a nation, nay a civilization, in return. No one has told us how we will tell the church school children that their families do not count.

There is no doubt about it. These calls to repentance are successful. They are successful in building walls and towers on top of seeds and flowers.

So go ahead and be unrepentant. The times in which we live require the cultivation of a graceful stubbornness. Do not apologize for it; it will stand us all in good stead. Refuse to be silenced! Despite the message of those good old days of yesteryear, silence is not golden. Refuse to be invisible. Hiding away gives in to the wishes of those who would have us disappear; it damages the movement for justice; it wounds our souls. Be proud of what you have accomplished in your life. Be proud of whom you love and whom you call family. The roots we have laid down give us strength.

BE OF GOOD FAITH

I struggle to be of good faith. Time and again, I am reminded that I am not alone. My communities of faith root me. The faith my parents continue to have in me reminds me that I am never alone. On August 8, 1998, at our "same-gender service," our network of biological and chosen family—ninety-six people strong—gave witness to the power of the gathered community. From the power of that gathered community, which represented so many different aspects of our lives, my life partner and I drew strength. We serve as reminders to others to be of good faith; they, in turn, serve as reminders to us to be of good faith. Therein lies our strength.

Remember that the religious right is not the only movement that has family values. Remember that those on the right are not the only ones with families. Know, too, that they are not the only ones whose intimate relationships are blessed by God. Know this well. Our families, of whatever configuration, are truly blessed. Our intimate relationships with each other are as holy as the sacrosanct relationship between one man and one woman for life. Remember that family values are not effective political rhetoric employed only by those who would condemn our families. Family values are part of our lives. We have family values. We show this every day in the ways that we care for one another. Family values get us through the good times and the bad. Ultimately, they nourish us and encourage us to reach out to others.

Be of good faith. Do not let the overwhelming nature of the struggle for justice dull your zest for life. Know that no one of us is expected to accomplish justice-love alone. Have faith that together we create, liberate, incarnate, and bless. Seek joy! Joy in the moment nurtures us. In the time of living in the not yet, relish the present. Ultimately, this moment is all we have. Be optimistic. Dance in the midst of unfinished business. Relish life. Love madly. Laugh loudly. And take it to the streets.

CULTIVATE A HOLY IMPATIENCE

Whoever said that patience was a virtue must have wanted control over impatient people. I am not talking here about the sort of impatience that city drivers show by blowing their horns before the traffic light has even changed. I am talking about the impatience that fuels our calls for justice. Impatience refuses to be told there is no way to turn injustice around. Impatience does not suffer fools gladly. Impatience refuses to be battened down, controlled, or molded. Impatience creates family out of no family; it creates a way out of no way; it creates hope out of no hope. As such, it is a holy thing indeed.

Holy impatience turns us around. It spurs our creative imaginations and renews us in the midst of struggle. It reminds us not to take ourselves so seriously that we lose sight of the larger picture. Holy impatience brings folks up short. Oftentimes, it helps others break through and see an issue in a way that no other patient and reasonable explanation would. Holy impatience breaks new ground. It reminds us that the Spirit among us is neither staid nor predictable. Holy impatience embraces the unexpected, forgets to be threatened, and throws caution to the winds. Often, this holy impatience will get us where we are going, even if we are convinced it is in the wrong direction.

Deep in my heart, I am an unrepentant, unapologetic agitator for justice-love in our most intimate relations, in our families, in our churches, and in our nation. Deep in my heart, I am of good faith: I trust that the bonds that connect me to my sister will never be wholly dissolved; I trust that I am not alone; I trust in an irrepressible joy of life to see us through. Deep in my heart, I rejoice in our holy impatience. I trust that with such vibrant, justice-loving cultivators of holy impatience, the struggle for liberation will never be dull.

Unrepentance, good faith, holy impatience—all of these stand us in good stead for times of trial and times of celebration. Be blessed and never stop blessing.

Notes

ACKNOWLEDGMENTS

1. The result of that panel was my article "Family Values Versus Valuing Families," *Journal of Feminist Studies in Religion* 12, no. 1 (spring 1996): 99–106.

AT THE CROSSROADS

1. Ralph Reed, former director of the Christian Coalition, takes exception to this and insists that no such judgment was ever intended. See Ralph Reed, *Active Faith: How Christians Are Changing the Soul of American Politics* (New York: Free Press, 1996). However, despite Reed's objections, the literature of the religious right is full of such references.

2. Robert H. Knight, *The Importance of Families and Marriage*, testimony on HB 609, HB 398, and HB 431 regarding marriage, workplace law, and "sexual orientation," at the Judiciary Committee, House of Delegates, State of Maryland (Washington, D.C.: Family Research Council, 1997).

3. Reed, *Active Faith*, 96.

4. The religious right in general seeks to distance itself from Christian reconstructionism, considered to be an extreme position (although many of Pat Robertson's views come perilously close to those of the movement). Those who advocate Christian reconstructionism believe that U.S. civil law should be modeled on biblical law. More specifically, advocates favor treating blasphemy, fornication, adultery, and homosexuality as crimes, with punishments encompassing imprisonment, beating, torture, and death.

Ralph Reed firmly disassociates the religious right from the reconstructionist movement and warns that its authoritarianism poses a threat to the well-being of a democratic society. Such theology, Reed warns his audience, cannot have any part in the theological justification of the political involvement of Christians. See Reed, *Active Faith*, 262.

For a recent treatment of white extremist groups, see Jerome Walters, *One Aryan Nation under God: Exposing the New Racial Extremists* (Cleveland: The Pilgrim Press, 1999).

5. Nelle Morton, *The Journey Is Home* (Boston: Beacon Press, 1985).

6. F. D. Maurice's use of "digging" as a metaphor for theologizing has always sparked my theological imagination. See Frederic Maurice, ed., *The Life of Frederic Denison Maurice*, vol. 11 (New York: n.p., 1884), 137.

7. The concept of "justice-love" was developed in the early 1990s by those working on a sexuality report for the Presbyterian Church (USA). See *Presbyterians and Human Sexuality* (Louisville: Office of the General Assembly, Presbyterian Church [USA], 1991), 9–10.

8. For a further elaboration of my methodological understanding of the processes of taking root and branching out, see my earlier book, *Eros Breaking Free: Interpreting Sexual Theo-Ethics* (Cleveland: The Pilgrim Press, 1995), 8–15.

1. THE ROOTS OF THE RELIGIOUS RIGHT

1. Jerry Falwell, 1995, as quoted on the jacket of William Martin, *With God on Our Side: The Rise of the Religious Right in America* (New York: Broadway Books, 1996).

2. Paul F. Knitter, *No Other Name? A Critical Survey of Christian Attitudes Toward the World Religions* (Maryknoll, N.Y.: Orbis Books, 1985), 76.

3. Ibid.

4. Nancy T. Ammerman, "North American Protestant Fundamentalism," in *Fundamentalisms Observed*, ed. Martin E. Marty and R. Scott Appleby (Chicago: University of Chicago Press, 1991), 4.

5. Clyde Wilcox, *Onward Christian Soldiers? The Religious Right in American Politics* (Boulder, Colo.: Westview Press, 1996), 27.

6. *The Fundamentals,* a collection of essays defending orthodoxy, was published in 1910. It provided the intellectual foundations, as well as the name, of the conservative religious movement, fundamentalism, which has manifested itself in the contemporary religious right.

7. Michael Lienesch, *Redeeming America: Piety and Politics in the New Christian Right* (Chapel Hill: University of North Carolina Press, 1993), 4.

8. Phillip E. Hammond, *The Protestant Presence in Twentieth-Century America* (Albany: State University of New York Press, 1992), 31.

9. Ronald C. White Jr. and C. Howard Hopkins, *The Social Gospel: Religion and Reform in Changing America* (Philadelphia: Temple University Press, 1976), xi.

10. Walter Rauschenbusch, excerpt from *Christianizing the Social Order* (1912), published in *Christian Social Ethics: A Reader*, ed. John Atherton (Cleveland: The Pilgrim Press, 1994), 176.

11. Martin E. Marty and R. Scott Appleby, *The Glory and the Power: The Fundamentalist Challenge to the Modern World* (Boston: Beacon Press, 1992), 53.

12. Quoted in William Martin, 13.

13. Ibid., 56.

14. Hammond, *Protestant Presence in Twentieth-Century America*, 38.

15. Billy Sunday, cited in George H. Williams and Rodney L. Petersen, "Evangelicals: Society, the State, the Nation (1925–75)," in *The Evangelicals*, ed. David F. Wells and John D. Woodbridge (Nashville: Abingdon Press, 1975), 219.

16. Martin, *With God on Our Side,* 9.

17. Lienesch, *Redeeming America,* 6.

18. Glenn H. Utter and John W. Storey, *The Religious Right: A Reference Handbook* (Santa Barbara, Calif.: ABC-CLIO, 1995), 4, 6.

19. Wilcox, *Onward Christian Soldiers?*, 34–35.

20. Billy James Hargis, *Christian Crusade Newspaper* 42 (August 1994), 1. See also Richard Hofstadter, *The Paranoid Style in American Politics and Other Essays* (New York: Vintage, 1966), 33–40.

21. Billy Graham, quoted in Martin, *With God on Our Side,* 33–34.

22. Falwell, quoted in Martin, *With God on Our Side,* 68–70.

23. David Edwin Harrel Jr., *Pat Robertson: A Personal, Religious, and Political Portrait* (New York: Harper & Row, 1987), 212.

24. Richard V. Pierard, "Religion and the New Right in Contemporary American Politics," in *Religion and Politics* (Waco, Tex.: Baylor University Press, 1983), 64.

25. Jerry Falwell, *How You Can Help Clean Up America* (Lynchburg, Va.: Liberty Publishing, 1978), 19.

26. Noted in David Harrel, "The Roots of the Moral Majority: Fundamentalism Revisited," in *Border Regions of Faith: An Anthology of Religion and Social Change*, ed. Kenneth Aman (Maryknoll, N.Y.: Orbis Books, 1987), 230.

27. Reed, *Active Faith*, 110.

28. Marty and Appleby, *Glory and the Power*, 70.

29. Lienesch, *Redeeming America*, 7.

30. Ibid., 74.

31. Both Jerry Falwell's Liberty University and Pat Robertson's Regent University were built then.

32. Jerry Falwell, *Listen, America!* (New York: Doubleday, 1980), 15–16.

33. Laurie Goodstein, "Religious Right Frustrated, Trying New Tactic on GOP," *New York Times,* March 23, 1998.

34. Weyrich cited in Richard Zone, "The Pro-Family Movement," *Conservative Digest*, May–June 1980, 15.

35. Quoted in Carolyn G. Heilbrun, *Reinventing Womanhood* (New York: Norton, 1979), 175.

36. Quoted in the *Houston Chronicle*, September 4, 1994, 20–21A.

37. Beverly W. Harrison, "The 'Fate' of the Middle Class in Late Capitalism," in *God and Capitalism: A Prophetic Critique of Market Economy*, ed. J. Mark Thomas and Vernon Visick (Madison, Wisc.: A-R Editions, 1991), 62–63.

38. Pat Robertson, "1997 Address to the Road to Victory Conference," transcript from 1997 annual meeting of the Christian Coalition, Washington, D.C.

39. Noted in Holly Sklar, "The Dying American Dream and the Snake Oil of Scapegoating," in *Eyes Right! Challenging the Right Wing Backlash*, ed. Chip Berlet (Boston: South End Press, 1995), 113.

40. Harrison, "'Fate' of the Middle Class," 64.

41. Ibid.

42. Elizabeth Bounds explores this in very helpful detail in "Between the Devil and the Deep Blue Sea: Feminism, Family Values, and the Division Between Public and Private," *Journal of Feminist Studies in Religion* 12, no. 1 (spring 1996): 112.

43. Ibid., 116.

44. Ibid., 117.

45. J. P. Wogaman, *Christian Perspectives on Politics* (Philadelphia: Fortress Press, 1988), 80.

46. Noted in Robert McAfee Brown, "The Religious Right and Political/Economic Conservatism," in *Border Regions of Faith*, 260.

47. Pat Robertson, "Is Capitalism Right or Wrong?" from the Web page of the Christian Broadcasting Network, August 1998, <www.cbn.org>.

48. Quoted in Wogaman, *Christian Perspectives on Politics*, 82.

49. Harrel, "The Roots of the Moral Majority," 240.

50. D. J. Gribbin, "Culture Cure," *Christian American*, March 1997.

51. Jerry Falwell, "A Biblical Plan of Action," in *Border Regions of Faith*, 245–46.

52. Pat Robertson, "Pat's Perspective: Is America Headed for Judgment?" on the Web page of *The 700 Club*, Christian Broadcasting Network, March 1998.

53. Ibid.

54. Falwell, "A Biblical Plan of Action," 250.

55. Sermon from 1949 entitled "Keepers of the Springs," by Peter Marshall, New York Avenue Presbyterian Church in Washington, D.C., quoted in Robert T. Handy, *A Christian America: Protestant Hopes and Historical Realities* (New York: Oxford University Press, 1971), 214–21.

56. Janet Fishburn, *Confronting the Idolatry of Family: A New Vision for the Household of God* (Nashville: Abingdon Press, 1991), 23.

57. Peter Marshall Jr., "Prodigal Nation—Part II," *Washington Watch* (Family Research Council) 9, no. 9 (July 1998): 6.

58. William Bennett, former secretary of education in the Reagan administration, quoted in Wilcox, *Onward Christian Soldiers?*

2. TO SAVE THE FAMILY

1. Testimony of Robert H. Knight, "The Importance of Families and Marriage," March 18, 1996, before the Senate Health, Education and Social Services Committee, State of Alaska, regarding SB 308, which would amend the state's marriage statute. From *At the Podium* (Washington, D.C.: The Family Research Council, March 22, 1996). Also available at their Web site, <http://www.frc.org/podium/pd96c1hs.html>.

2. Ralph Reed, *Politically Incorrect: The Emerging Faith Factor in American Politics* (Dallas: Word, 1994), 91.

3. Ibid., 264.

4. Jerry Falwell, "An Agenda for the Eighties," in *The Fundamentalist Phenomenon: The Resurgence of Conservative Christianity*, ed. Jerry Falwell with Ed Dobson and Ed Hindson (Garden City, N.Y.: Doubleday, 1981), 205.

5. Adam Meyerson, "Family. Faith. Freedom: How Conservatives Can Set the Cultural Agenda," *Policy Review: The Journal of American Citizenship*, no. 83 (May–June 1997): 99.

6. Reed, *Active Faith*, 5.

7. Pat Robertson, "1997 Address to the Road to Victory Conference."

8. "About the Christian Coalition," from the Christian Coalition Web page.

9. Reported in Robert Boston, *The Most Dangerous Man in America? Pat Robertson and the Rise of the Christian Coalition* (Amherst, N.Y.: Prometheus Books, 1996), 87.

10. Reported in ibid., 96. The Christian Coalition was under investigation by the Internal Revenue Service for possible violations of its tax-exempt status. (Tax-exempt religious organizations are to maintain political neutrality.) In June 1999 its tax-exempt status was revoked.

11. October 1998 fund-raising letter for the Christian Coalition signed by Randy Tate.

12. Senators Trent Lott and Mitch McConnell, speeches given at the Christian Coalition's Road to Victory Conference, Washington, D.C., September 18, 1998.

13. From the Christian Coalition Web site, "About the Christian Coalition" and "Christian Coalition's 5-Fold Mission."

14. Ibid., "About the Christian Coalition."

15. Statement by Ralph Reed Jr., executive director (at the time) of the Christian Coalition, on the occasion of the release of the "Contract with the American Family," May 17, 1995.

16. Ibid.

17. The Christian Coalition's "Contract with the American Family," as reproduced on the Christian Coalition Web site.

18. Reed, *Active Faith*, 153.

19. Ralph Reed, "Casting a Wider Net: Religious Conservatives Move Beyond Abortion and Homosexuality," *Policy Review* (summer 1993): 33.

20. Laurie Goodstein, "Religious Right Frustrated, Trying New Tactic on GOP."

21. Press release, "'Families 2000' Strategy Announced by Christian Coalition. State and National Leaders Plan Future of Coalition," from the Christian Coalition Web page, February 18, 1998.

22. Ibid.

23. "Christian Coalition in Disarray," in *Freedom Writer* (March/April 1999): 1–2. (Published by the Institute for First Amendment Studies, Great Barrington, Mass.)

24. "About Us" from the Christian Broadcasting Network Web page.

25. "Who Is AFA?" from the official Home Page of the American Family Association, Inc., August 1998, <http://www.afa.net>.

26. "Who Is Don Wildmon?" from the official Home Page of the American Family Association, Inc., August 1998.

27. Donald E. Wildmon, "Shall We Have Respectability at the Loss of Responsibility?" *American Family Association Journal* (June 1998): 2.

28. Ironically, Cyber Patrol, one of the largest Internet-filtering software packages, blocked the Web site for the American Family Association (AFA), citing the fact that information provided in opposition to the lesbian/gay movement is "intolerant" and legitimates discrimination on the basis of sexual orientation. In turn, the AFA responded, complaining that it was the victim of religious discrimination.

29. "Does AFA Hate Homosexuals?" and "Does AFA Support Censorship?" from the official Home Page of the American Family Association, Inc., August 1998.

30. Statistics taken from "American Family Association" on "Who's Who on the Religious Right," People for the American Way Web site, <http://www.pfaw.org/issues/right/bg_groups.shtml#afa>.

31. Reed, *Active Faith*, 266.

32. Quoted in Ami Neiberger, "Promise Keepers: Seven Reasons to Watch Out," *Freedom Writer*, Institute for First Amendment Studies (November 1996): 3; originally quoted in the *Los Angeles Times*.

33. From the official Web site of the Promise Keepers, <http://www.promisekeepers.org>.

34. Noted in Ken Abraham, *Who Are the Promise Keepers? Understanding the Christian Men's Movement* (New York: Doubleday, 1994), 166.

35. Loretta J. Williams, "Some Promises Not to Keep," *Unity First*, August 1997, 1.

36. Richard Morin and Scott Wilson, "Men Were Driven to 'Confess Their Sins': In Survey, Attendees Say They Are Also Concerned about Women, Politics," *Washington Post*, October 5, 1997, A19.

37. From the official Web site of the Promise Keepers, <http://www.promisekeepers.org/21ca.htm>.

38. "Protecting the Rights of the Family through Prayer and Action," from the Web site of Concerned Women for America, <http://www.cwfa.org/about.html>.

39. Quoted in Leon Howell, *Funding the War of Ideas* (Cleveland: United Church Board for Homeland Ministries, 1995), 27.

40. See Carter Heyward and Anne Gilson, eds., *Revolutionary Forgiveness: Feminist Reflections on Nicaragua* (Maryknoll, N.Y.: Orbis Books, 1986).

41. Re-Imagining, a global ecumenical conference, was held in November 1993 in Minneapolis. It was first planned as an event to celebrate the World Council of Churches' Ecumenical Decade: Churches in Solidarity with Women, and the purpose was to bring women theologians, clergy, and laypersons together to do theology from women's experience. The event caused a major backlash among conservative organizations that denounced the conference, urged churches to withhold moneys from denominational events, called for church leaders to resign, and urged the censure of future feminist/womanist/*mujerista* activities. See Nancy J. Berneking and Pamela Carter Joern, *Re-Membering and Re-Imagining* (Cleveland: The Pilgrim Press, 1995), especially xv–xvii.

42. "IRD Questions Claims on Black Church Fires," *United Voice* 8, no. 6 (December 1996): 6–7.

43. The address, 475 Riverside Drive, is the location of the Interchurch Center in New York City, which houses the World Council of Churches, the National Council of Churches, and the denominational headquarters of the United Methodist Church. The building used to house the denominational headquarters of the United Church of Christ, which moved to Cleveland, Ohio, and the Presbyterian Church (USA), which moved its headquarters to Louisville, Kentucky. Quoted in Howell, *Funding the War of Ideas*, 35.

44. Quoted in Howell, *Funding the War of Ideas*, 35–36.

45. Janice Shaw Crouse, Diane LeMasters Knippers, and Alan Wisdom, eds., *A Christian Women's Declaration* (Washington, D.C.: Ecumenical Coalition on Women and Society and Institute on Religion and Democracy), 9–11.

46. Leslie Zeigler, Professor of Christian Theology, Emerita, Bangor Theological Seminary, United Church of Christ, quoted in ibid., 13.

47. Ibid., 7.

48. Ibid.

49. Ibid.

50. Charmaine Crouse Yoest, political commentator and columnist, quoted in ibid., 14.

51. "Promise Keepers Growing," *New York Times Magazine,* April 27, 1997, 28.

52. "Promise Keeper's Organizations for Women Are Founded," *Good News Magazine,* January 1, 1998, 3.

53. Quoted on the Web site for the National Organization for Women, "Myths and Facts about the Promise Keepers," July 1998, <http://www.now.org/issues/right/promise/mythfact.html#goodforwomen>.

54. Quoted in Gloria Goodale, "Faith and Family Are Chosen Track for 'Chosen Women,'" *Christian Science Monitor,* April 1997, 16.

55. Ibid.

56. "Where Does Women for Faith and Family Stand on Issues of Concern to Me?" from the Women for Faith and Family Web site, August 1998, <http://www.catholicity.com/cathedral/womenff/WFFQA.html#Six>.

57. Faye Short, "Bold Women," *Good News: A Magazine for United Methodist Renewal,* July–August 1998, 39.

58. Quoted in Howell, *Funding the War of Ideas,* 28–29.

59. From "Our Guiding Principles" on the Focus on the Family Web site, <http://www.family.org/welcome/aboutfof/a0000078.html>.

60. James Dobson, "Summary of Comments Made During the White House Briefing on the Family," January 17, 1984, 2, posted on the Focus on the Family Web site.

61. Ibid., 4.

62. Quoted in Howell, *Funding the War of Ideas,* 28.

63. From "Who's Who on the Religious Right" on the People for the American Way Web site.

64. From the Family Research Council Web page, July 1998, <http://www.frc.org>.

65. Ibid.

66. From "Who's Who on the Religious Right" on the Web site of People for the American Way.

67. Jerry Falwell, "Southern Baptist Revolution Continues," *Falwell Fax,* June 12, 1998.

68. Marie Griffith and Paul Harvey, "Wifely Submission," *Christian Century,* July 13, 1998, online version, <www.christiancentury.org>.

69. James V. Heidinger II, "The Conversations We Aren't Having," *Good News,* September–October 1998, 9.

70. Ibid.

71. "The History of the Presbyterian Lay Committee," from the Web site of the *Presbyterian Layman,* <http://www.layman.org>, 1.

72. Ibid., 2. See also my book, *Eros Breaking Free.*

73. "Parker T. Williamson: Slain Missionaries Defining Moment for Layman Editor," from the Web site of the *Presbyterian Layman,* 2.

74. Todd Wetzel, executive director of Episcopalians United, in the *1997 Annual Report*.

75. The Episcopalians United Mission Statement.

76. "Survey of Christian Right Activists," the Bliss Institute of the University of Akron in cooperation with the Institute for First Amendment Studies, 1997. Of the 1,200 activists contacted, 600 responded, representing a cross section of 200,000 to 400,000 Americans. From the Institute for First Amendment Studies Web site, <www.ifas.com>.

3. THREATENED BY CHAOS, SAVED BY TRADITION

1. Gary Bauer, *Our Hopes, Our Dreams: A Vision for America* (Colorado Springs: Focus on the Family, 1996), 14.

2. James Dobson, *From Dr. James Dobson* (newsletter), June 1998, 5.

3. Bill McCartney at a 1992 press conference, quoted in Abraham, *Who Are the Promise Keepers?*, 25.

4. Alan Keyes, a speech given at the Christian Coalition's Road to Victory Conference, Washington, D.C., September 18, 1998.

5. Carmen Pate of Concerned Women for America, a workshop on traditional marriage at the Christian Coalition's Road to Victory Conference, Washington, D.C., September 19, 1998.

6. Reggie White, quoted in "NFL Star Sacked for Christian Views," *American Family Association Journal*, June 1998, 4.

7. Pat Robertson, remarks made on *The 700 Club*, reported by Mark Lane, "Smiting Disney World with Meteor More Precise Than with Hurricane," *Daytona Beach News-Journal*, June 16, 1998.

8. "Today, on 'The 700 Club' Pat Robertson Said His Comments on Orlando's Gay Days Events Were Misrepresented and Taken Out of Context," CBN press release, June 10, 1998.

9. Resolution passed during the Southern Baptist Convention in Salt Lake City in June 1998. Quoted in *SBC Bulletin*, Report of Committee on Resolutions, Southern Baptist Convention, June 9–11, 1998.

10. Ibid.

11. Robert H. Knight, director of cultural studies at the Family Research Council, "Statement on National Coming Out of Homosexuality Day," at a press conference, October 10, 1996.

12. Ibid.

13. Dobson, *From Dr. James Dobson*, June 1998, 1.

14. Ibid., 3–4.

15. Comments made by Anthony Falzarano, executive director of Transformations Ex-Gay Ministry, during "Same-Sex Marriage? Straight Talk from the Family Research Council," broadcast aired Wednesday, April 10, 1996. Transcribed by Joyce McPhee.

16. The full-page advertisements, sponsored by a coalition of fifteen organizations including the Christian Coalition, the Family Research Council, Concerned

Women for America, and the American Family Association, appeared in the *New York Times* (July 13, 1998), the *Washington Post* (July 14, 1998), and *USA Today* (July 15, 1998). Television advertisements were aired in October 1998.

17. Anthony Falzarano, "The Defense of Marriage Act: An Insider's View," speech at Capitol Hill briefing concerning the Defense of Marriage Act (DOMA), July 2, 1996, sponsored by the Family Research Council.

18. Anthony Falzarano, quoted in "Religious Leaders Expose Hypocrisy Behind the Religious Right's Anti-Gay National Ad Campaign and Warn Republicans," press release by the Interfaith Alliance, July 15, 1998.

19. Falzarano, "The Defense of Marriage Act," July 2, 1996.

20. Reed, *Active Faith*, 265–66.

21. See William Martin, *With God on Our Side: The Rise of the Religious Right in America* (New York: Broadway Books, 1996), 248.

22. Scott Ross, "The Not So Gay Way: Out of the Closet," *CBN Online*, from the Web site <www.700club.org>, May 1998, 2.

23. "Why Pro-Family Groups Oppose Domestic Partner Benefits," *American Family Association Journal*, April 1998, 7.

24. "Lawfully Wedded?" *Family Voice* (Concerned Women for America), April 1996, 3.

25. Testimony of Robert H. Knight, "The Importance of Families and Marriage," March 18, 1996.

26. Daniel P. McGivern, president, Hawaii Christian Coalition, message sent to all subscribers to the Christian Coalition E-mail news list, July 22, 1998.

27. "Homosexuality in America: Exposing the Myths," on the Web page of the American Family Association, August 1998.

28. Quoted in Caryle Murphy, "Christian Groups' Ad Hits a Raw Nerve," *Washington Post*, July 19, 1998, B1.

29. Beverly LaHaye, quoted in Lienesch, *Redeeming America*, 72.

30. James C. Dobson, *Straight Talk to Men and Their Wives* (Waco, Tex.: Word, 1980), 69, 155.

31. Ibid., 155.

32. Midge Decter, "Family," Heritage Foundation Twenty-fifth Anniversary Leadership for America Lectures, Denver, Colorado, July 9, 1998.

33. Tony Evans, *No More Excuses: Be the Man God Made You to Be* (Wheaton, Ill.: Crossway Books, 1996), 185.

34. Reed, *Politically Incorrect*, 83.

35. Patrick F. Fagan, "Social Breakdown in America," in *The Candidate's Briefing Book* (Washington, D.C.: Heritage Foundation, 1996), 11.

36. Pat Robertson, *The Turning Tide: The Fall of Liberalism and the Rise of Common Sense* (Dallas: Word, 1993), 180–81, 302.

37. Robert Rector, "Welfare: Expanding the Reform," in *Issues '98: The Candidate's Briefing Book* (Washington, D.C.: Heritage Foundation, 1998), 1.

38. Lucy Williams, *Decades of Distortion: The Right's 30-Year Assault on Welfare* (Somerville, Mass.: Political Research Associates, 1997), 1.

39. "The Family: Preserving America's Future," excerpts from the *Report to the President from the White House Working Group on the Family*, *Phyllis Schlafly Report*

21, no. 7 (1988). See also "The Family's Stake in Economic Policies," *Phyllis Schlafly Report* 18, no. 9 (April 1985): 1, 3–4.

40. Gary Bauer, "The Family: Preserving America's Future," *Report to the President from the White House Working Group on the Family* 24 (1986).

41. Almost always this rise in illegitimacy is attributed to African Americans. See Robert Rector, "Welfare Reform and the Death of Marriage," *Washington Times,* February 23, 1996, A20.

42. Williams, *Decades of Distortion*, 12.

43. Rector, "Welfare: Expanding the Reform," 23.

44. Focus Group Report by Public Agenda for the Kaiser Family Foundation, quoted in "Immigration and Welfare: The Politics of Resentment," *Radical America* 26, no 1 (1995): 4.

45. *Gary Bauer's Monthly Letter* (Family Research Council), July 1998, 1.

46. Ibid.

47. Karl Day, "Cardinal Virtues: 4+1=0," *American Family Association Journal*, June 1998, 20–21. Reprinted from *Washington Watch*, a publication of the Family Research Council.

48. James Dobson, *Family News from Focus on the Family*, July 1998, 7.

49. Berit Kjos, "From Father God to Mother Earth: The Effect of Deconstructing Christian Faith on Sexuality," *Theology Matters* (a publication of Presbyterians for Faith, Family and Ministry) 3, no. 5 (September–October 1997): 4.

50. Knight, "Statement on National Coming Out of Homosexuality Day," October 10, 1996.

51. "Spin Cycle: Propaganda and the Homosexual Movement," Family Research Council, Washington, D.C., July 1998.

52. Kjos, "From Father God to Mother Earth," 8.

53. Reed, *Active Faith*, 9–10.

54. Ibid., 256.

55. *Murphy v. Ramsey*, Supreme Court decision, 1885, quoted in "The Importance of Families and Marriage," testimony of Robert H. Knight, March 18, 1996. See also *SBC Bulletin*, Baptist Faith and Message "Family" Article, Southern Baptist Convention, June 9–11, 1998.

56. Lienesch, *Redeeming America*, 52–53.

57. Beverly LaHaye, quoted in Martin, *With God on Our Side*, 178.

58. Dobson, *Straight Talk*, 21.

59. From an *American Family Association Action Letter*, January 1998.

60. Knight, "Same-Sex Marriage? Straight Talk from the Family Research Council."

61. Patrick Fagan of the Heritage Foundation, a workshop on traditional marriage at the Christian Coalition's Road to Victory Conference, Washington, D.C., September 19, 1998.

62. Patrick Fagan, "The Breakdown of the Family: The Consequences for Children and American Society," in *Issues '98: The Candidate's Briefing Book* (Washington, D.C.: Heritage Foundation, 1998), 19.

63. Reed, *Politically Incorrect*, 258–59.

64. *SBC Bulletin*, Report of Committee on Resolutions, Southern Baptist Convention, June 9–11, 1998.

65. Testimony of Robert H. Knight, "The Importance of Families and Marriage," March 18, 1996.

66. *SBC Bulletin*, Baptist Faith and Message "Family" Article, Southern Baptist Convention, June 9–11, 1998.

67. Crouse et al., *A Christian Women's Declaration*, 3.

68. From the Family Research Council Web page, "The Importance of Families and Marriage," testimony of Robert H. Knight before the Judiciary Committee, House of Delegates, State of Maryland, on HB 609, HB 398, and HB 431, regarding marriage, workplace law, and "sexual orientation," March 12, 1997.

69. Ibid.

70. Hadley Arkes, "The Implications of Gay 'Marriage,'" speech given at a Capitol Hill briefing on the Defense of Marriage Act (DOMA), July 2, 1996, sponsored by the Family Research Council.

71. Reed, *Active Faith*, 266.

72. Dobson, *Straight Talk*, 21–22.

73. Ibid., 23.

74. Reported in Boston, *The Most Dangerous Man in America?*, 163.

75. Bill McCartney, interview on National Public Radio, October 1, 1997.

76. Timothy LaHaye, quoted in Lienesch, *Redeeming America*, 54–55.

77. Phyllis Schlafly, *The Power of the Christian Woman* (Cincinnati, Ohio: Standard Publishing Company, 1981), 24–27.

78. Tim LaHaye, *How to Be Happy Though Married* (Wheaton, Ill.: Tyndale House, 1968), 57, 63.

79. Lienesch, *Redeeming America*, 57.

80. LaHaye, *Happy Though Married*, 29.

81. *Seven Promises of a Promise Keeper* (Colorado Springs: Focus on the Family Publishing, 1994), 73–74.

82. LaHaye, *Happy Though Married*, 106. See also Beverly LaHaye, *The Restless Woman* (Grand Rapids, Mich.: Zondervan, 1984), 128.

83. Dobson, *Straight Talk*, 157.

84. Charles Stanley, *A Man's Touch* (Wheaton, Ill.: Victor Books, 1977), 116.

85. Bob Green, quoted in Anita Bryant, *Bless This House* (Old Tappan, N.J.: Revell, 1972), 143.

86. *SBC Bulletin*, Baptist Faith and Message "Family" Article, Southern Baptist Convention, June 9–11, 1998.

87. *Seven Promises of a Promise Keeper*, 79.

88. Quoted in *Church and State*, October 1993, 20.

89. Quoted in John D. Spalding, "Bonding in the Bleachers: A Visit to the Promise Keepers," *Christian Century*, March 6, 1996, 261–62.

90. Dobson, *Straight Talk*, 154.

91. Beverly LaHaye, *The Restless Woman*, 73, and *I Am a Woman by God's Design* (Old Tappan, N.J.: Revell, 1980), 29.

92. Midge Decter, "Family," July 9, 1998.

93. Reported in Dobson, *Family News from Focus on the Family*, July 1998, 3.

94. See my earlier book, *Eros Breaking Free*, especially 31–36, 55–57 for an in-depth analysis of how the complementarity theory has shored up the theological justification of restrictive gender roles.

95. Schlafly, *The Power of the Christian Woman*, 48, 75.

96. Lienesch, *Redeeming America*, 70–71.

97. Tim LaHaye, quoted in ibid., 74.

98. James C. Dobson, *Love for a Lifetime* (Portland, Oreg.: Multnomah Press, 1987), 45–46.

99. Henry Hyde, "A Mom and Pop Manifesto: What the Pro-Family Movement Wants from Congress," *Policy Review* (spring 1994): 30.

100. Ibid.

101. Reed, *Politically Incorrect*, 83.

102. Ibid., 86.

103. Ibid., 258.

104. Rector, "Welfare: Expanding the Reform," 17.

105. Pamela K. Brubaker, "Making Women and Children Matter: A Feminist Theological Ethic Confronts Welfare Policy," in *Welfare Policy: Feminist Critiques*, ed. Elizabeth Bounds, Pamela K. Brubaker, and Mary Hobgood (Cleveland: The Pilgrim Press, 1999), 13.

106. Myron Magnet, *The Dream and the Nightmare: The Sixties' Legacy to the Underclass* (New York: William Morrow, 1993), 16.

107. Representative Tom DeLay, speech at the Christian Coalition's Road to Victory Conference, Washington, D.C., September 18, 1998.

108. Beverly LaHaye, quoted in *Ms Magazine*, February 1987, 34.

109. The Council for National Policy was founded by fundamentalist psychologist Tim LaHaye. It is a council of key leaders of the political and the religious right, which meets to discuss strategy on national policy issues.

110. Even though this project does not cover the far right Christian reconstructionist movement, it is important to report Howard Phillips's views since he addressed the Council for National Policy meeting, which is made up of the major leaders of the religious and the political right.

111. Howard Phillips, speech to the Council for National Policy, 1998, from the Institute for First Amendment Studies Web site, <http://www.berkshire.net/~ifas>.

112. Quoted in Justin Watson, *The Christian Coalition: Dreams of Restoration, Demands for Recognition* (New York: St. Martin's Press, 1997), 93.

113. Pat Robertson, "Morality and Justice: Law Must Embrace Morality," speech at William and Mary Law School, February 23, 1995. Published in *Christian American*, April 1995.

114. Pat Robertson and Ralph Reed, speeches at the Christian Coalition's Road to Victory Conference, Washington, D.C., September 18, 1998.

115. Chuck Colson, speech at the Christian Coalition's Road to Victory Conference, Washington, D.C., September 19, 1998.

116. Frederick Clarkson, "PK's Promise—A Christian Nation?" *Center for Democracy Studies: PK Watch*, no. 1 (March 1997): 1.

117. Ibid.

118. Quoted in Watson, *The Christian Coalition*, 95.

119. Pat Robertson, "Faith and Democracy," *Christian American*, November–December 1993, 16.

120. Ralph Reed Jr., "What Religious Conservatives Really Want," in *Disciples and Democracy*, ed. Michael Cromartie (Washington, D.C.: Ethics and Public Policy Center, 1994), 3–4.

121. Pat Robertson, *Pat Robertson's Perspective* (newsletter), April–May 1992.

122. Reed, *Active Faith*, 120.

123. Pat Robertson, fund-raising letter, July 4, 1991.

124. Pat Robertson, "Pat Robertson's Perspective," *Christian American*, October–November 1992.

125. Rabbi Daniel Lapin, speech at the Christian Coalition's Road to Victory Conference, Washington, D.C., September 18, 1998.

126. Don Hodel, at presentation in honor of Pat Robertson during the banquet at the Christian Coalition's Road to Victory Conference, Washington, D.C., September 19, 1998.

127. Charlton Heston, keynote address during the banquet at the Christian Coalition's Road to Victory Conference, Washington, D.C., September 19, 1998.

128. Donald E. Wildmon, "Shall We Have Respectability at the Loss of Responsibility," *American Family Association Journal*, June 1998, 2.

129. Virginia L. Thomas, quoted in Crouse et al., *A Christian Women's Declaration*, 13.

130. Bill McCartney, speech at Promise Keepers' 1996 Clergy Conference, Atlanta, Georgia, February 14, 1996. Quoted in Abraham, *Who Are the Promise Keepers?*, 169.

131. Tim Kingston, "Blueprint for Hate: Contents of Secret Colorado Anti-Gay Election Kit Revealed," *San Francisco Bay Times*, May 19, 1994, 3.

132. See Boston, *The Most Dangerous Man in America?*, 109.

133. Dobson, *Family News from Focus on the Family*, July 1998, 5.

134. Reed, *Politically Incorrect*, 42, 50.

135. Robertson, *The Turning Tide*, 301–16.

136. Pat Robertson, "Morality and Justice: Law Must Embrace Morality."

137. Dobson, *Family News from Focus on the Family*, July 1998, 7.

138. Quoted in "Thought Police Pursuing Dissidents," *American Family Association Journal*, August 1998, 10.

139. Gary L. Bauer, "Testimony on the Defense of Marriage Act" (S. 1740), July 11, 1996, before the United States Senate Judiciary Committee.

140. Quoted in "Congress Should Say No to Special Rights for Homosexuals, FRC Says," Family Research Council press release, July 27, 1998.

141. Watson, *The Christian Coalition*, 130.

142. Bill McCartney, quoted in Nancy Novosad, "God Squad: The Promise Keepers Fight for a Man's World," *The Progressive*, August 1996, 25.

143. Reed, *Active Faith*, 256.

144. Crouse et al., *A Christian Women's Declaration*, 8.

145. Pat Robertson, "1997 Address to the Road to Victory Conference."

146. Reed, *Politically Incorrect*, 222–23.

147. Reed, introduction to *Contract with the American Family* (Nashville: Moorings, 1995), ix–x.

148. Cited in Religious News Service dispatch, May 15, 1990, and quoted in Boston, *The Most Dangerous Man in America?*, 90.

149. Ralph Reed, speech at the Christian Coalition's Road to Victory Conference, Washington, D.C., September 18, 1998.

150. Dobson, *From Dr. James Dobson*, June 1998, 8.

4. WHOSE FAMILY? WHOSE FAITH? WHAT JUSTICE?

1. James Dobson and Gary Bauer, 1990, quoted on the PBS Web page for *God on Our Side*.

2. Quoted in Lienesch, *Redeeming America*, 77.

3. Personal conversation with Janis Costas, August 1998. She has delightfully described the nature of God as being "wildly inclusive."

4. See my earlier book, *Eros Breaking Free*.

5. Marvin M. Ellison, *Erotic Justice: A Liberating Ethic of Sexuality* (Louisville, Ky.: Westminster John Knox Press, 1996), 17.

6. Reed, *Politically Incorrect*, 10.

7. Sister Maureen Fieldler, a Roman Catholic nun in the order of the Sisters of Loretto and Co-coordinator of the Quixote Center, quoted in "Religious Leaders Expose Hypocrisy Behind the Religious Right's Anti-Gay National Ad Campaign and Warn Republicans," press release from the Interfaith Alliance, July 15, 1998.

8. See, for example, Katie G. Cannon, *Katie's Canon: Womanism and the Soul of the Black Community* (New York: Continuum, 1995); Elisabeth Schüssler Fiorenza, *In Memory of Her: A Feminist Theological Construction of Christian Origins* (New York: Crossroad, 1983); and Letty M. Russell, *Household of Freedom: Authority in Feminist Theology* (Philadelphia: Westminster Press, 1987).

9. Angie Warren, quoted in the *Washington Post*, October 5, 1997, A16.

10. Robertson, *The Turning Tide*, 185.

11. LaHaye, *Happy Though Married*, 29.

12. Robertson, *The Turning Tide*, 185.

13. *Seven Promises of a Promise Keeper*, 73–74.

14. James Dobson, quoted in *Church and State*, October 1993, 20.

15. See David Blankenhorn, *Fatherless America* (New York: Basic Books, 1995). He directs the National Fatherhood Initiative (see the Web site <www.fatherhood.org>). See also the National Center for Fathering <www.fathers.com/infox.html>.

16. Judith Stacey, *In the Name of the Family: Rethinking Family Values in the Postmodern Age* (Boston: Beacon Press, 1996), 35.

17. Crouse et al., *A Christian Women's Declaration*, 7.

18. Ibid., 5–6.

19. Midge Decter, "Family," July 9, 1998.

20. Much ink has been spilled regarding these questions. The purpose here is not so much to lay out the evidence that would argue against distinct gender-based roles as it is to raise key questions that later become the basis for constructive alternatives to the proposals of the religious right. See, for instance, Carol P. Christ and Judith Plaskow, eds., *Womanspirit Rising: A Feminist Reader in Religion* (New York: Harper & Row, 1979); Simone de Beauvoir, *The Second Sex: The Classic Manifesto of the Liberated Woman* (New York: Vintage Books, 1952); Vivian Gornick and Barbara K. Moran, eds., *Woman in Sexist Society: Studies in Powerlessness* (New York: Basic Books, 1971); bell hooks, *Feminist Theory: From Margin to Center* (Boston: South End Press, 1984); Rosemary Radford Ruether, ed., *Religion and Sexism: Images of Women in the Jewish and Christian Traditions* (New York: Simon & Schuster, 1974); and Barbara Smith, ed., *Home Girls: A Black Feminist Anthology* (New York: Kitchen Table: Women of Color Press, 1983).

21. See my earlier book, *Eros Breaking Free*, for a more detailed description of the complementarity theory.

22. Dobson, *From Dr. James Dobson*, June 1998, 1.

23. Blankenhorn, *Fatherless America*, 233.

24. Ellison, *Erotic Justice*, 18.

25. See the discussion on moral panics in ibid., 17–19.

26. Ibid., 20.

27. McGivern, message sent to all subscribers to the Christian Coalition E-mail news list, July 22, 1998.

28. Alan Keyes, speech at the Christian Coalition's 1998 Road to Victory Conference, September 18, 1998. The transcript is available at the Christian Coalition's Web site, <http://www.cc.org/rtv98/speeches/keyes.html>.

29. Fagan, a workshop on traditional marriage at the Christian Coalition's Road to Victory Conference, Washington, D.C., September 19, 1998.

30. Knight, "The Importance of Families and Marriage," March 12, 1997.

31. Ellison, *Erotic Justice*, 84.

32. Carole R. Bohn, "Dominion to Rule: The Roots and Consequences of a Theology of Ownership," in *Christianity, Patriarchy, and Abuse*, ed. Joanne Carlson Brown and Carole R. Bohn (New York: The Pilgrim Press, 1989), 105.

33. Ibid., 107.

34. Susan E. Davies, "Reflections on the Theological Roots of Abusive Behavior," in *Redefining Sexual Ethics: A Sourcebook of Essays, Stories, and Poems*, ed. Susan E. Davies and Eleanor H. Haney (Cleveland: The Pilgrim Press, 1991), 57.

35. Mary Hobgood, "Marriage, Market Values, and Social Justice: Toward an Examination of Compulsory Monogamy," in *Redefining Sexual Ethics*, 116.

36. Decter, "Family," July 9, 1998.

37. Robertson, *The Turning Tide*, 172.

38. Decter, "Family," July 9, 1998.

39. Stacey, *In the Name of the Family*, 10.

40. *The Compact Edition of the Oxford English Dictionary* (Oxford: Clarendon Press, 1971).

41. Ibid.

42. See discussion in Stacey, *In the Name of the Family*, 39–40.

43. See discussion in Paula Giddings, *When and Where I Enter . . . : The Impact of Black Women on Race and Sex in America* (New York: William Morrow, 1984), 41–43.

44. Quoted in Lienesch, *Redeeming America*, 77.

45. Karen L. Bloomquist, "Sexual Violence: Patriarchy's Offense and Defense," in *Christianity, Patriarchy, and Abuse*, 63.

46. Ibid., 65.

47. Ibid., 65–66.

48. Suzanne Pharr, *In the Time of the Right: Reflections on Liberation* (Berkeley, Calif.: Chardon Press, 1996), 11–38.

49. Reported in Stacey, *In the Name of the Family*, 10.

50. Reed, *Politically Incorrect*, 86.

51. Rector, "Welfare: Expanding the Reform," 1.

52. Ibid., 8.

53. Julian Shipp, "Panelists Discuss Effects of Welfare from Many Perspectives," *PCUSA News*, November 4, 1997.

54. Quoted in "Join 'The National Day of Action for Welfare/Workfare Justice,'" the Interfaith Alliance Web page, November 28, 1997, <http://www.tialliance.org>.

55. Ibid.

56. Rector, "Welfare: Expanding the Reform," 6.

57. C.R. Windegarden, "AFDC and Illegitimacy Ratios: A Vector Autoregressive Model," *Applied Economics* (March 1988): 1589–1601. Cited in Rector, "Welfare: Expanding the Reform," 9.

58. Cited in Rector, "Welfare: Expanding the Reform," 9.

59. Stacey, *In the Name of the Family*, 47.

60. Pharr, *In the Time of the Right*, 15.

61. Robertson, "1997 Address to the Road to Victory Conference." Jerry Falwell described capitalism as "God's plan for our economy," quoted in Brown, "The Religious Right and Political/Economic Conservatism," 260.

62. Bounds, Brubaker, and Hobgood, *Welfare Policy: Feminist Critiques*, 3.

63. Pharr, *In the Time of the Right*, 22.

64. Jerry L. Van Marter, "Welfare Consultation Participants Hear Firsthand Stories," *PCUSA News*, November 4, 1997.

65. Reed, *Politically Incorrect*, 83.

66. See Pamela K. Brubaker's estimation of this in "Making Women and Children Matter: A Feminist Theological Ethic Confronts Welfare Policy," in *Welfare Policy: Feminist Critiques*, 14–15.

67. Dorothy Roberts, "The Value of Black Mothers' Work," *Radical America* 26, no. 1 (1996): 10.

68. Lucy Williams, *Decades of Distortion*, 1.

69. Roberts, "Value of Black Mothers' Work," 13.

70. Fagan, "Social Breakdown in America," 2.

71. Dr. James Allen Fox, dean of the College of Criminal Justice at Northeastern University, Boston, Massachusetts, quoted in Fagan, "Social Breakdown in America," 8.

72. Fagan, 10–11.

73. Judith Stacey treats this phenomenon in some historical detail. See Stacey, *In the Name of the Family*, 73 f.

74. From the official Promise Keepers Web site.

75. Equal Partners in Faith has done extensive work on the Promise Keepers and other issues regarding the religious right. The group can be reached in care of Lafayette Avenue Presbyterian Church, 85 South Oxford Street, Brooklyn, New York 11217. Telephone (718) 625-7515; fax (718) 797-4556.

76. Joe Conason, Alfred Ross, and Lee Cokorinos, "The Promise Keepers Are Coming: The Third Wave of the Religious Right," *Nation*, October 7, 1996, 14–16.

77. Quoted in *Colorado Springs Gazette Telegraph*, June 18, 1996.

78. David A. Love, "Keeping Watch on the Promise Keepers," *Emerge Magazine*, April 1997, 1.

79. Loretta J. Williams, "Some Promises Not to Keep," *Unity First*, August 1997, 1.

80. Press Fact Sheets from Equal Partners in Faith.

81. Watson, *The Christian Coalition*, 3.

82. Robertson, "Morality and Justice: Law Must Embrace Morality."

83. Dobson, *Family News from Focus on the Family*, July 1998, 7.

5. FAITH, FREEDOM, AND FAMILY

1. Reed, *Active Faith*, 30.

2. "That Cause Can Neither Be Lost nor Stayed," in *The Cokesbury Worship Hymnal* (New York: Abingdon-Cokesbury Press, 1938), 169, stanza 1.

3. Morton, *The Journey Is Home*.

4. The Rev. Dr. C. Welton Gaddy in a press release by the Interfaith Alliance, July 1998.

5. Carter Heyward, *The Redemption of God* (Lanham, Md.: University Press of America, 1982), 153.

6. Shared by the Rev. Elizabeth Alexander, in personal correspondence, August 25, 1998.

7. Personal correspondence from John S. Carter, August 3, 1998.

8. Personal correspondence from Angela Bauer, Ph.D., August 11, 1998.

9. Personal correspondence from Jason Abbott, Ph.D., August 5, 1998.

10. The Greenfire Community, in Tenant's Harbor, Maine, was founded in 1991 by four women Episcopal priests as a women's retreat center.

11. Personal correspondence from the Rev. Dr. Alison Cheek, August 4, 1998.

12. Personal correspondence from Reed Franklin, August 3, 1998.

13. Personal correspondence from Beverly Ward, August 3, 1998.

14. Personal correspondence from Michele C. Sherman, August 10, 1998.

15. Personal correspondence from Meg Gorsline, August 15, 1998.

16. Conversation with the Rev. Dr. Judith A. Davis, October 1998.

17. Conversation with Dr. Chung Hyun Kyung, New York City, May 1998.

18. Personal correspondence from Joan M. Sakalas, August 3, 1998.

19. Personal correspondence from Kathryn Easton, Ph.D., August 11, 1998.

20. Personal correspondence from Pamela K. Brubaker, Ph.D., August 3, 1998.

21. Personal correspondence from Jann Craig, August 8, 1998.

22. "That Cause Can Neither Be Lost nor Stayed," stanza 2.

23. Carter Heyward, *Staying Power: Reflections on Gender, Justice, and Compassion* (Cleveland: The Pilgrim Press, 1995), 5–6.

24. Carter Heyward, *Our Passion for Justice: Images of Power, Sexuality, and Liberation* (New York: The Pilgrim Press, 1984).

25. I cannot think of anyone who has influenced me more on the topic of relationality than Carter Heyward. Surely, this is evident in her writings. But it has been most apparent to me in our friendship of more than sixteen years. I cannot write about the subject of relationality without acknowledging her influence.

26. Charlton Heston, keynote address at the banquet for the Christian Coalition's 1998 Road to Victory Conference, September 19, 1998.

27. Delores Williams, "A Womanist Perspective on Sin," in *A Troubling in My Soul: Womanist Perspectives on Evil and Suffering*, ed. Emilie M. Townes (Maryknoll, N.Y.: Orbis Books, 1993), 145–46.

28. Carter Heyward, *Saving Jesus from Those Who Are Right* (Minneapolis: Fortress Press, 1999).

29. "That Cause Can Neither Be Lost nor Stayed," stanza 3.

30. Heyward, *Staying Power*, 118.

31. Pharr, *In the Time of the Right*, 90.

32. Ada María Isasi-Díaz, *Mujerista Theology: A Theology for the Twenty-first Century* (Maryknoll, N.Y.: Orbis Books, 1996), 89.

33. Audre Lorde, "The Transformation of Silence into Language and Action," in *Sister Outsider* (Trumansburg, N.Y.: The Crossing Press, 1984), 41.

CONCLUSION

1. "That Cause Can Neither Be Lost nor Stayed," stanza 4.

Index

134, 194 nn. 6, 143, 146–49, 196 nn. 50, 65, 197 n. 1. *See also* Christian Coalition

Re-Imagining Ecumenical Women's Conference, 48, 51, 58, 186 n. 41; and Ecumenical Coalition on Women and Society, 49–50; and Institute on Religion and Democracy, 48

relativism, 72–73. *See also* tolerance

Religious Freedom Amendment, 39, 41, 145

Religious Roundtable, 23–24

Riverside Church, 154, 164

Robertson, Pat, 23, 25–27, 30, 32, 64, 80, 89–92, 94–97, 108–10, 124, 145, 170, 181 n. 4, 183 n. 38, 184 nn. 7, 47, 52, 188 nn. 7–8, 189 n. 36, 192 nn. 113–14, 193 nn. 119, 121, 123–24, 135–36, 194 nn. 10, 12, 145, 195 n. 37, 196 n. 61, 197 n. 82; and Christian Broadcasting Network, 41–42; and Promise Keepers, 45; and 700 Club, 42. *See also* Christian Coalition

Schlafly, Phyllis, 25, 71, 80–81, 85, 190 n. 39, 191 n. 77, 192 n. 95

school prayer, 21, 31, 39, 54, 89

secular humanism, 22–23, 31, 48

sexuality, 73–74, 81. *See also* complementarity theory; lesbian and gay issues; marriage, covenant; marriage, traditional

social construction theory, 8–9, 49

Social Gospel Movement, 17–18, 20, 75; and Walter Rauschenbusch, 17–18, 182 n. 10

socialism, 30–31

Southern Baptist Convention, 56–57, 64, 77, 85, 188 nn. 9–10, 191 nn. 64, 66, 86. *See also* male headship; submission, female

Stacey, Judith, 110, 134, 194 n. 16, 195 n. 39, 196 nn. 42, 49, 59, 197 n. 73

submission, female, 51, 68, 80, 83–86, 109–11, 121–22, 127–28, 187 n. 68; and Promise Keepers, 45; and Southern Baptist Convention, 56–57. *See also* male headship

Sunday, Billy, 20, 182 n. 15

superiority, ethics of, 134, 136, 138–39, 141, 146–47

tolerance, 73–74, 123. *See also* relativism

Traditional Values Coalition, 55; and Louis Sheldon, 55

United Methodist Church, 57; and Good News, 51, 187 n. 57; and Good News Renewal, 57; and Re-Imagining Ecumenical Women's Conference, 51; and Renew, 51–52

unwed mothers, 34, 44, 70–72, 86–87, 131, 133, 139. *See also* welfare

victimization, 144–46, 173. *See also* Watson, Justin

Watson, Justin, 144–45. *See also* victimization

welfare, 7, 29, 31, 39, 70–72, 86–88, 117, 130–40, 189 nn. 37–38; and Aid to Families with Dependent Children, 71; behavioral poverty, 131–32, 135–36; and Henry Hyde, 86; and racism, 71; and War on Poverty, 131–33; and Welfare Reform Act of 1996, 87; and workfare, 132, 134, 138

Williams, Delores, 169, 198 n. 27

Women for Faith and Family, 51

World Council of Churches, 20

Praise for
The Battle for America's Families

———

"This book brings the reader to the edge of the deep chasm that runs through American Protestantism. Standing on the side of feminist and liberation theology with its commitment to love and social justice, Anne Gilson looks across the canyon toward the religious right with its attachment to divine judgment, punishment, and control. It is a rift that runs through her own family of origin and has moved her to become part of a family of a different kind. The book is like a letter to people on her side in need of insight, encouragement, and affection. A humane work, filled with keen understanding of God's love and America's predicament."

—Tom F. Driver, Paul Tillich Professor of
Theology and Culture Emeritus,
Union Theological Seminary,
New York, and author of
*Liberating Rites: Understanding
the Transformative Power of Ritual*

"THE BATTLE FOR AMERICA'S FAMILIES is an indispensable guide for anyone wishing to enter the 'family values' debate in support of an inclusive, justice-seeking model of families. Not only offering a clear and concise overview of a range of groups on the Christian right, Gilson speaks compassionately about the fears behind the attacks on feminists, gays, single mothers, and others who are considered "anti-family." Especially helpful is her explanation of the way that gay rights, marriage, racism, and welfare policy are all part of the battle for 'family values.' By recasting the theological assumptions underlying the Christian Right's model of the family, Gilson offers us a positive vision of a just creation which needs to be heard."

—Elizabeth M. Bounds, Associate
Professor of Christian Ethics,
Candler School of Theology,
Emory University, Atlanta,
and author of *Coming Together,*
Coming Apart: Religion,
Community, and Modernity

"Those who mistakenly dismiss the religious right as simply misguided or underestimate its control agenda should stop everything and read Anne Gilson's glistening analysis of the 'pro-family' movement, its central players, and its ideology. More troubling than we often take in, the religious right has fueled the cultural backlash against feminism, gay civil rights, welfare, and anti-racism politics. Gilson's critique is crisp and fair. Her constructive response is principled, timely, and compassionately drawn. This is an important work by a next-generation feminist theologian whose own family values embrace the contradictions she so ably describes."

—Marvin Ellison, Bass Professor of Ethics,
Bangor Theological Seminary,
Bangor, Maine, and author of
Erotic Justice: A Liberating
Ethic of Sexuality

"In THE BATTLE FOR AMERICA'S FAMILIES, Anne Gilson not only calls for a cease-fire between the religious right and religious feminists but starts the peace talks. Motivated by the damage this battle has done to her biological family, Gilson has written a poignant and accessible investigation to counter 'snobby,' liberal dismissals of the religious right. She shows how 'the family' serves as foot soldier and tells stories of families gone AWOL from the battle. This is a book about diverse families' values."

—Kathleen Greider, Associate Professor of Pastoral Care and Counseling, Claremont School of Theology, Claremont, California, and author of *Reckoning with Aggression: Theology, Violence, and Vitality*